Nature: The Mirror of Being

Dr. Virendra Kumar Shekhar

DIAMOND BOOKS
www.diamondbooks.in

Publisher	**:**	**Diamond Pocket Books (P) Ltd.** X-30, Okhla Industrial Area, Phase-II, New Delhi-110020
Phone	:	011-40712200
E-mail	:	wecare@diamondbooks.in
Website	:	www.diamondbooks.in
Edition	:	2026
Printed By	:	Repro (India)

Nature: The Mirror of Being

Author - *Dr. Virendra Kumar Shekhar*

If You Wish So...*Nature shows you the path to becoming the best version of yourself*

Foreword

It gives me great pleasure to pen a few words about the latest book authored by the versatile and deeply insightful writer, Dr. V. K. Shekhar, IPS (Retd.).

It is widely known that Dr. Shekhar is a gifted writer, poet, and artist. However, this newest work of his reveals something even deeper—his profound reverence for timeless wisdom and eternal truths.

This book is a remarkable contribution that transcends the boundaries of gender, age, or religion. The eternal teachings of the Mahabharata and the Gita have been skillfully woven into its pages, offering readers valuable guidance on how to maintain inner balance and meet life's inevitable ups and downs with equanimity, resilience, and courage.

Dr. V. K. Shekhar has beautifully explained the holistic nature of human existence—highlighting that true harmony lies not only in balancing body, mind, and soul, but also in aligning oneself with one's surroundings, the environment, and the larger rhythms of nature.

One of the most powerful messages of this book is the infallibility of the human spirit and the immense potential with which every individual is endowed by the Divine. And if someone falls short of realizing their full potential, the fault often lies not within the individual, but in the external ecosystem, circumstances, and environment in which they are placed.

This book serves as a self-help roadmap for anyone who wishes to grow, evolve, and find peace within. I am deeply impressed by Dr. Shekhar's clarity of philosophical insight and his ability to make profound truths accessible, enjoyable, and meaningful to the average reader.

Heartiest congratulations, dear Dr. Shekhar.

- Dr. Vikram Singh IPS (Retd.)
Ex DGP (U.P.)

Preface

Brahman is both *Vyakta* (manifest) and *Avyakta* (unmanifest), and yet transcends both; hence it is called *Parama Brahman.*

To express the *Avyakta*, we have assumed the form of *Vyakta*. What is this *Avyakta*? To what extent are we able to express it in our lives?

And why must the unmanifest be manifested at all? To find answers to these questions, *Ātma-bodha*—the awakening of the Self—is most essential and indispensable.

According to the author of this book, "Self-realization is the very purpose of life."

In the Indian philosophical vision, particularly in the *Yoga Darśana* of Maharshi Patanjali, *Vyakta* represents *Prakriti*—the changing, perishable, and mutable reality. The awareness and constant experience of the Eternal not only establish us in our true, immutable essence (what is called *Sthitaprajñatā*, or inner stability) but also enable us to act in the transient and perishable world with detachment, awareness, and skill.

The purification of *Chitta* (mind-stuff) and the transformation of consciousness toward its original and truthful nature constitute the process and endeavor known as spiritual practice.

To abide in one's essential nature is to be established in truth—this indeed forms the foundation of the soul's journey through life.

The book begins with a profound and meaningful assertion:

"We are not a coincidence but a purpose."

Upon reading this in the introduction, the reader immediately perceives the author's clarity of thought and depth of vision.

What is the purpose of human existence? What means and methods must one adopt to advance toward that purpose? What obstacles arise on the path, and how are they to be overcome?

It is the author's deep contemplation on the truth of human existence that forms the central theme of this book.

With remarkable clarity and insight, the author has expressed subtle and profound spiritual wisdom in a manner that is both simple and deeply relevant to modern human life. His book offers ideas that are not only practical and experiential but also profoundly transformative for physical, mental, social, and spiritual development.

Such reflection, writing, and reading are not merely inspirational—they are timeless, enlightening, and immensely useful, forming the very foundation for the transformation of consciousness.

With heartfelt joy and deep respect, I extend my warmest congratulations and best wishes to Dr. V. K. Shekhar, a thinker of rare insight, luminous intellect, and inner quest.

I also offer my affectionate good wishes to all fellow travelers on this journey of self-evolution.

The continuous journey—from self-forgetfulness to self-remembrance, from *Ātman* to *Paramātman*, from the Supreme Person of the *Bhagavad Gītā* to the ideal human of the *Rāmāyaṇa*, and to the *Puruṣottama* of the *Yoga Darśana*—is nothing but the movement toward one's own supreme form.

And as the author beautifully expresses:

"Reaching one's highest self is not a destination but a continuous journey."

This thought reveals the author's clear and purposeful vision.

—Āchārya Neeraj Yogi
President, Yoga Bhārati East, Rishikesh (Uttarakhand)

Author's Note

In the Mahabharata, both Duryodhana and Arjuna faced inner turmoil at some occasions—but the way they responded made all the difference between self-destruction and self-realization. Duryodhana's famous words to Krishna in the Udyog Parva (43.58) capture a deep moral conflict:

"जानामि धर्मं न च मे प्रवृत्ति : । जानाम्यधर्मं न च मे निवृत्तिः ।।"

"I know what is Dharma, yet I do not act accordingly. I know what is Adharma, yet I cannot restrain myself."

Here, Duryodhana openly confesses his awareness of right and wrong, but simultaneously admits his helplessness before his inner compulsions.

However, what is more tragic is not his weakness—but his unwillingness to seek a way out of it. He accepts his tendencies as unchangeable destiny, blaming his nature (Svabhava) rather than taking responsibility. He neither seeks guidance nor aspires to rise above his inner conflict. This fatal passivity leads him to ruin.

In contrast, Arjuna, in the Bhagavad Gita (2.7), also suffers a moral breakdown on the battlefield. But instead of surrendering to despair or ego, he surrenders to wisdom. He says:

"शिष्यस्तेऽहं शाधि मां त्वां प्रपन्नम्"

"I am your disciple. Teach me, for I have taken refuge in you."

Arjuna's surrender is not weakness—it is the gateway to spiritual awakening. By acknowledging his confusion and seeking knowledge from Krishna, he opens himself to transformation.

The entire Bhagavad Gita becomes a dialogue of enlightenment because Arjuna dared to ask and to learn.

Thus, both characters knew Dharma, but one sought liberation while the other clung to ego. The lesson is clear:

"Awareness is not enough—true wisdom lies in the humility to seek guidance and the courage to transform."

Introduction

In every human heart lies a yearning — sometimes voiced, often veiled — to grow, to rise, to become better than before. Yet, as the days rush past in the monotony of routines and the burden of struggles, one may pause and wonder: "Why should I strive to become the best version of myself? Isn't mere survival enough? Why reach beyond what already is?"

This question does not stem from laziness or rebellion; it is a philosophical inquiry, a deeply human reflection. To answer it is to enter into the very essence of life, identity, and growth. For the pursuit of becoming our best self is not merely a personal ambition — it is an existential necessity, an obligation to ourselves, to others, and to the vast, intricate web of life.

Unlike stones or machines, we are not born finished; we are born as possibilities. A tree sleeps within a seed, called forth by light and soil. In the same way, each human life carries within it the capacity to evolve — physically, intellectually, emotionally, morally, and spiritually. Growth is the very language of life. The body heals its wounds; the mind stretches toward understanding; the heart seeks ever-deeper connection; the soul hungers for meaning. To resist this current is to resist life itself. As the Buddha has beautifully said, *"What you are is what you have been; what you will be is what you do now."* To strive toward your best self is nothing less than aligning yourself with the river of life that flows toward fullness.

Many mistake the call to their best self as a demand for external success — wealth, fame, or power. Yet, true striving is not about comparison, not a competition played out on the world's stage. It is about an inner alignment, a quiet integrity, a sacred fulfillment. When you labor to unfold your potential, you enter a state where effort becomes effortless — the state of flow. When your deeds mirror your values, you taste peace. When your life radiates what you most deeply believe, fulfillment blooms within. No amount of accolades can replace the quiet, golden certainty that you have lived sincerely, fully, and purposefully.

At any given moment, life offers each of us but one chance — one mind, one body, one breath. To drift through this gift without striving to polish and lift ourselves is to squander something irreplaceable. Your body, capable of strength and grace — would you leave it weak and untested? Your mind, able to think, imagine, and create — would you abandon it to distractions and dullness? Your emotions, born to nurture and heal — will you let them corrode in jealousy and anger? Your life, capable of radiating light — will you let it pass unshaped in shadows? You owe it to yourself to find out what you can become. You owe it to your own soul.

When you grow, you do not grow alone. The ripple of your effort spreads outward, touching others. Personal growth, far from being selfish, is the highest form of service. A more patient parent, a more empathetic friend, a more visionary leader, a more honest citizen, a more compassionate human being — these are the gifts your better self bestows upon the world. Remember those teachers who awakened you, those healers who mended you, those poets who stirred your heart. Their greatness enriched you. Your personality, if nurtured, will enrich others as well.

Becoming the best version of yourself is not a destination to reach, but a path to walk. Each day is an opportunity — to learn one new truth, to replace one harmful habit, to offer one kind word, to choose courage over comfort. It is not about grand victories, but about the patient artistry of becoming. You need not be perfect; you need only to keep moving forward. Progress, however modest, transforms life into a pilgrimage — meaningful not because it is easy, but because it is true.

A sculptor does not see only a block of stone; he sees the figure slumbering within. Likewise, within you is a masterpiece awaiting your hand — not shaped by fate or chance, but by your conscious choices. You will not become your best self by accident, but by intention. Not by shortcuts, but by steadfast sincerity. Not by dreams alone, but by daily action. Every choice is a brushstroke upon the canvas of your life. Will you let the picture be random, or will you craft it with deliberation and love?

Life is unpredictable. No one knows how many days they are given, what storms may come, what fortunes may fall away. Yet, one thing remains steadfast: your effort. To strive to be your best self is the only endeavor whose rewards are imperishable. It fortifies you in adversity, prepares you for opportunity, and weaves a legacy that lingers long after you are gone. Though you cannot control all that befalls you, you can shape who you become in response.

Strangely, it is not in stillness but in striving that we find out who we are. We discover ourselves not in the absence of struggle but in the midst of it — in the falling, the rising, the enduring. As the Bhagavad Gita urges: *"Uddhared atmanātmānaṁ"* — lift yourself by yourself. In striving toward your highest self, you peel away ignorance, illusion, and fear. What remains is not a false personality, but the pure, aware, capable essence you were always meant to embody.

The world today teeters under the weight of countless challenges — moral confusion, ecological crisis, social division, technological dilemmas. In these turbulent times, we need not just more knowledge but more wisdom; not just more cleverness but more consciousness. We need individuals of integrity, clarity, compassion, and strength. Your best self is not a private luxury; it is a public necessity. When individuals lift themselves, families heal, communities strengthen, and nations rise.

In the end, you will regret not what you tried and failed, but what you never dared to attempt. Why should you strive to become the best version of yourself? Because you were born to grow. Because that growth infuses life with meaning. Because you are capable of far more than you now believe. Because others are waiting — consciously or not — for your light. Because the future you, looking back, will offer thanks. Because there is no nobler pursuit. Do not wait for the perfect moment or the ideal circumstance. Begin now, with what you have, where you are. As has been wisely said: Success is not being better than someone else; it is being better than who you were yesterday.

This question — "Why should I try to become the best version of myself?" — is more than a call to action; it is a philosophical inquiry, one that has echoed through the corridors of Indian thought for millennia. It is not answered by mere motivation, but by profound reflections on the true nature of existence. Indian philosophy teaches us that we are not random accidents, but bearers of the eternal Self (*Ātman*), expressions of the cosmic reality (*Brahman*), and participants in the sacred dance of life (*Purushartha*).

In this grand vision, striving to become our best self is not about personal ambition or vanity. It is *Dharma* (Righteousness) — a sacred duty. Endowed with *Viveka* (discrimination between important and unimportant), through *Vairagya* (dispassion from unimportant) driven by *Mumukshutva* (the longing for liberation), we are called not merely to exist, but to awaken. Self-realization is not an ornament to life; it is its very purpose.

Buddha's teachings, too, affirm that striving for the highest is not a glorification of ego, but a liberation of the heart and mind from the chains of suffering. The path is not pride but Dhamma — the patient cultivation of *sīla* (ethics), *samādhi* (concentration), and *paññā* (wisdom). It is a compassionate, courageous journey from darkness into light, from fear into fearlessness, from delusion into awakening.

This effort — to become the best version of yourself — is not optional. It is the essence of what it means to be human. It is the timeless summons to live not merely as a creature of habit, but as a conscious artist shaping the masterpiece of a life well-lived.

Contents

Chapter-1

Personality is the outward reflection of an individual's inner being

It is not limited to external appearances but is rooted more deeply in the values, thoughts, and emotions that shape behavior and action. A common misconception equates personality with appearance—the way one dresses, speaks, or carries themselves. Yet, these visible aspects are merely the tip of the iceberg. The deeper and more enduring elements lie within: in the values one upholds, the thoughts one cultivates, and the discipline one practices.

In truth, the external expression is a mirror of the internal state. A calm, confident, and ethical individual naturally radiates a charm and dignity that no amount of cosmetics or stylish attire can fabricate. Real personality development, therefore, requires an integrated approach that nurtures not just the body but also the senses and the mind.

Human beings interact with the world through three primary instruments: the senses (*indriyas*), the mind (*manas*), and the body (*sharira*). For holistic personality development, conscious and systematic refinement of all three is essential. Human existence is not isolated; it is a dynamic relationship with the environment and others, mediated by the senses, the mind's interpretations, and the body's actions and expressions. Neglecting any one of these aspects results in imbalance—leading either to excessive inwardness and detachment or to superficial and reactive behavior. True development demands an integrated strategy.

The senses serve as the gateways to the external world. Through sight, hearing, smell, taste, and touch, they gather information and deliver it to the mind. The state of the senses influences the impressions we absorb and, by extension, the personality we project. Cultivating sensory awareness is the first step toward refinement. Most people use their senses passively, overwhelmed by the barrage of stimuli. Developing awareness involves training the eyes to notice details, patterns, and subtleties; listening actively to capture not just words but emotions and intentions; savoring flavors and aromas mindfully; and cultivating sensitivity in touch, fostering empathy and emotional intelligence. Enhanced sensory awareness deepens engagement with the world, enriches communication, and renders interactions more meaningful.

Yet, awareness alone is not enough; discipline of the senses is equally crucial. Unchecked sensory indulgence leads to distraction, restlessness, and even addiction. Ancient Indian philosophy emphasizes *indriya nigraha*—training the senses to serve higher purposes rather than allowing them to dictate the mind's path. Practical steps include avoiding overstimulation by regulating exposure to noise and excessive media consumption; choosing wholesome sights, sounds, and environments that uplift the mind; and resisting temptations that lead to indulgence in food, luxury, or entertainment. Mastery over the senses endows an individual with composure, grace, and focus, contributing to a personality marked by clarity and poise.

Beyond the senses lies the mind—the central processing unit of personality. The mind interprets sensory inputs, stores experiences, forms beliefs, generates emotions, and directs actions. A refined mind is the foundation of a refined personality. Developing emotional intelligence becomes vital here. Understanding, managing, and expressing emotions appropriately enhances interpersonal effectiveness. Emotional intelligence encompasses self-awareness, the recognition of one's emotions and their effects; self-regulation, managing emotions constructively; empathy, the ability to sense and understand others' emotions; and social skills that foster positive relationships based on respect and trust. Those endowed with emotional intelligence exhibit patience, compassion, and resilience. They remain calm under pressure and navigate conflicts with grace—qualities that form the bedrock of a magnetic personality.

Integral to the mind's refinement is the building of a strong value system. Values like honesty, integrity, respect, and humility form the inner compass that determines authenticity. External charm, without a sturdy value system, is hollow and transient. Values must be chosen consciously and internalized through regular reflection on beliefs and actions, learning from role models who exemplify integrity, and maintaining consistency in aligning actions with values, even under adversity. An individual grounded in strong values radiates trustworthiness and commands respect.

Equally important is the cultivation of cognitive abilities. A sharp, agile mind adds brilliance to personality. Developing skills such as critical thinking, problem-solving, and creativity ensures intellectual vibrancy. This can be achieved by reading widely across diverse fields, engaging in meaningful dialogue and debates to refine articulation and clarity, and practicing mindfulness to enhance concentration and clear mental clutter. A mind so developed reflects intelligence and wisdom, making the individual not only engaging but also influential.

Thus, personality, though often misunderstood as merely external appearance, is in essence the harmonious expression of a refined inner being through the senses, the mind, and the body. When nurtured consciously, it becomes a natural, compelling force—an outward manifestation of inner strength, clarity, and grace.

The body is the medium through which all expressions of personality are made visible. It reflects the mind's state and showcases one's self-discipline, habits, and energy. Good health forms the foundation of a dynamic and attractive personality. A healthy body ensures energy, stamina, and a vibrant presence. Regular physical activity improves posture, vitality, and resilience. A balanced diet nourishes not just the body but also supports mental clarity, while adequate sleep and relaxation are critical for recovery and balance. A person who cares for their body communicates discipline and self-respect, naturally commanding respect from others.

Though substance outweighs style in importance, appearance cannot be neglected. Grooming and presentation are outward expressions of self-care and respect for others. Cleanliness and neatness signal responsibility; Appropriate, well-fitted clothing boosts confidence and leaves positive impressions. Body language — through posture, gestures, eye contact, and facial expressions — silently conveys much about an individual's inner state. A composed, clean, and confident demeanor enhances the overall impact of one's personality.

The discipline required to maintain physical health mirrors the discipline needed for mental and emotional refinement. Regular routines cultivate perseverance, punctuality, and reliability — qualities that are highly valued in both professional and personal life. Individuals with disciplined lifestyles tend to be more organized, goal-oriented, and dependable, naturally enhancing their credibility and influence.

Each dimension — senses, mind, and body — is deeply interconnected. Neglecting one impairs the others. Poor health of the body can lead to irritability of the mind, and overindulgence of the senses can weaken concentration and sap physical energy. Integrated development is, therefore, key to a complete personality. Balanced engagement of the senses leads to clarity of mind, resulting in purposeful action. A healthy body supports a vigorous mind, which in turn enables effective communication. A disciplined mind refines the senses and fosters graceful body language. A truly developed personality emerges when the senses are keen but disciplined, the mind sharp yet compassionate, and the body energetic and well-maintained — all working together in seamless harmony.

To nurture this integration, practical strategies are necessary. A daily mindfulness practice, even of just 10–15 minutes, helps in observing thoughts and emotions without judgment. Moderating sensory inputs by reducing unnecessary exposure to noise, excessive screen time, and indulgent entertainment preserves mental clarity and focus. Maintaining a physical routine that includes exercise, a balanced diet, and sufficient rest strengthens the body's resilience.

Continuous learning through reading, engaging in meaningful dialogues, and exposing oneself to diverse ideas sharpens the intellect. Regular reflection on core values ensures that belief and behavior are consistently aligned. Grooming habits — including personal hygiene, appropriate dressing, and mindful body language — enhance outward expression. Engaging in acts of service cultivates empathy and diminishes self-centeredness. Setting realistic, meaningful goals fosters continuous improvement across the dimensions of senses, mind, and body.

Personality is far more than what meets the eye. While the outer appearance forms one facet, the lasting and impactful dimensions of personality reside in the values, emotions, discipline, and habits an individual cultivates. The outer look, in truth, is but a reflection of the inner qualities that radiate through it.

A person's interaction with the world is mediated through the senses, mind, and body. Holistic personality development, therefore, requires: conscious effort to refine sensory perceptions, cultivate mental discipline and emotional intelligence, and maintain physical fitness and grooming. By nurturing all three aspects in harmony, individuals can evolve into balanced, graceful, and resilient personalities — ones that not only succeed outwardly but also carry the inner light of wisdom, empathy, and authentic strength. Such a personality transcends mere impressions; it inspires, leaving a positive impact that lingers long after the individual has passed by.

❐

Chapter-2

You are an Important Constituent of Nature

From the first breath we take to the last, human beings remain inseparable from nature. We are not external observers of the natural world; we are intricately woven into its fabric. Every cell in our body, every rhythm in our life, reflects deeper laws that silently govern the universe. Despite our towering technological advancements, we are perpetually bound by the natural laws that crafted us. Understanding and observing nature is not a mere intellectual pastime; it is a transformative journey toward aligning ourselves with the fundamental truths that sustain life. In this alignment lies the secret to cultivating a resilient, adaptive, and harmonious personality.

Nature, in its quiet majesty, presents a vast web of interconnected systems. Trees, rivers, soil, air, and animals do not exist in isolation; they thrive because of their **interdependence.** The flourishing of one form of life is intricately tied to the health of another. Similarly, a personality cannot blossom in isolation. **Empathy, cooperation, and mutual respect** become essential traits. Recognizing our dependence on others nurtures emotional intelligence and broadens our social adaptability. It teaches us that **meaningful connections** are the lifeblood of human existence.

Adaptability is another profound lesson nature imparts. Species that survive are not the strongest, but those most flexible in adapting to change. Nature's silent endorsement of **flexibility and resilience** is a timeless lesson. In a rapidly shifting world, those who embrace change, who weather adversity with courage, develop a strength of character that stands unshaken. Mental flexibility, **openness to new experiences,** and the **ability to navigate setbacks** are invaluable assets in the cultivation of a complete personality.

Nature is not static; it pulses with cycles and rhythms. Day and night, seasons, tides, birth and death — all are part of its grand design. These are not disruptions but necessary patterns that facilitate

renewal and growth. Human development too follows cycles: periods of intense activity must be balanced with rest, triumph often follows failure, and sorrow paves the way for joy. Accepting these natural oscillations helps us foster **patience** and a profound understanding of growth.

Balance is another hallmark of nature. Ecosystems seek **equilibrium;** predator and prey, rain and drought, creation and destruction are all harmoniously balanced. For individuals, balance manifests in harmonizing ambition with humility, discipline with flexibility, and **logic with emotion**. A balanced personality is not lopsided but is instead a confluence of seemingly opposite traits working in tandem.

Each organism in nature has a unique **purpose**. Bees pollinate flowers, earthworms aerate the soil, and rivers carve out landscapes. Purpose is not an accidental byproduct; it is intrinsic. When individuals discover their unique purpose, their lives gain direction and meaning. Purpose fuels resilience and ignites motivation. It transforms ordinary existence into **intentional living,** where every action aligns with a greater mission.

Nature favors **simplicity and efficiency**. Trees reach upward, rivers carve the simplest paths, and animals conserve energy for survival. **Complexity often leads to chaos and confusion.** By simplifying our goals, focusing on what truly matters, and **eliminating distractions,** we increase our effectiveness and foster **inner contentment.**

Adversity is not alien to nature. Forests regenerate after fires, muscles grow stronger under stress, and the lotus blooms in muddy waters. Similarly, personal growth often roots itself in hardship. **Challenges are not obstructions** but stepping stones that build **resilience.** Learning to view obstacles as opportunities for self-betterment is a hallmark of a mature personality.

No two leaves are identical; biodiversity ensures **the robustness of ecosystems.** Nature thrives on diversity. Likewise, **human uniqueness is not a flaw but a strength.** Embracing individuality rather than imitating others cultivates authenticity. It encourages us to appreciate the diversity around us, fostering a **spirit of acceptance and understanding.**

Nature constantly renews itself. Animals hibernate, trees shed leaves, rivers cleanse themselves. For humans, **continuous self-renewal** is vital. **Periodic reflection, lifelong learning, and mental rejuvenation** prevent stagnation and foster vitality. **Letting go of burdens from the past** clears the way for future growth.

True strength in nature is often silent. Mountains stand firm without boast; rivers shape landscapes through persistent, quiet flow. **True human strength also lies not in noise but in quiet confidence and humility**. A personality built on humility and steadfastness commands genuine respect and admiration.

Nature is full of **symbiotic relationships.** Bees and flowers, fungi and trees — species **cooperate for mutual benefit.** Similarly, in human life, **teamwork and cooperation** often achieve what solitary effort cannot. **Sharing knowledge, resources, and embracing win-win paradigms** enriches all involved.

Conservation is a principle woven deeply into nature. Animals conserve energy for survival, trees conserve water by shedding leaves. Humans, too, must learn to **conserve emotional and mental energy**. **Focusing on meaningful tasks, avoiding unnecessary drains, and knowing when to act and when to retreat are vital strategies for an efficient and purposeful life.**

Nature shows the wisdom of surrender. Rivers do not battle rocks; they flow around them. Trees bend with the wind to avoid breaking. Acceptance is not defeat but intelligent adaptation. **When we accept what cannot be changed and work harmoniously with challenges rather than against them, we grow stronger and wiser.**

Nature is ever-present. Trees do not dwell on the past, nor do rivers worry about the future. They exist in the "now." Similarly, mindfulness brings focus, calmness, and self-awareness. **Living in the present moment** reduces anxiety and cultivates a deeper engagement with life's experiences.

Nature sustains itself through **recycling and renewal. Waste from one organism becomes nourishment for another**. **Sustainability** is not an option but a necessity. For individuals, **sustainable habits and responsible behavior** ensure long-term happiness and societal well-being. **Living responsibly, thinking beyond immediate gains, and fostering habits that contribute to collective welfare mark a mature personality.**

Ultimately, we are born from nature and dwell within its grand design. To live meaningfully, we must recognize that the principles governing trees, rivers, stars, and creatures are the very laws that govern us. By observing and internalizing these principles, we can align our personality development with the profound wisdom embedded in the natural world.

Nature teaches us **interdependence, resilience, balance, and purposeful living.** It instills in us **patience, silence, cooperation, and sustainability.** If we listen carefully and learn humbly, we can cultivate a personality that is not only successful but deeply harmonious with the universe.

Thus, the journey toward a refined, evolved personality is not a distant quest; it is intimately woven into the simple, eternal lessons of nature. All that is required is the humility to observe, the wisdom to understand, and the courage to apply these lessons in daily life.

Nature, the eternal teacher, awaits those who are willing to learn. *"Look deep into nature, and then you will understand everything better."* — Albert Einstein

❐

Chapter-3

Nature grants all the chance to grow and evolve—some seize it and shine, others let it slip and fade

Nature, in its vast expanse and intricate design, extends care and provision to every living being, regardless of size, strength, or significance. From the mightiest elephant to the tiniest microbe, every organism is woven into the fabric of life, each granted the means for survival and the opportunity for growth. This universal nurturing is not merely accidental but embedded into the very laws of existence, demonstrating that nature is not indifferent but deeply attentive. With adaptability and a conscious intention to adopt and evolve, living beings can harness this nurturing power to enhance their quality of life and longevity.

Nature ensures that every creature, howsoever tiny or huge, is endowed with resources suitable for its sustenance and growth. Plants receive sunlight, water, and soil nutrients; animals are granted instinct, mobility, and appropriate habitats; microorganisms thrive in environments invisible to the naked eye. This intricate system is a balanced web, where every life form plays a role and receives what is necessary for its existence. For example, the humble ant, often overlooked, has food sources, shelters, and mechanisms to adapt to seasonal changes. On the grander scale, the elephant is provided with vast forests and water bodies essential for its sustenance. Even in harsh terrains like deserts or polar regions, life persists and flourishes within the limits nature defines, exhibiting its impartial care.

A deeper look reveals that nature operates on principles of balance and interdependence. No creature lives in isolation; every being is part of a larger, dynamic ecosystem. The bee pollinates the flower while seeking nectar; the trees purify the air while taking in carbon dioxide exhaled by animals. This reciprocity ensures not only the survival of individuals but the continuity of life itself. It is crucial to understand that this balance is delicate.

When one species grows unchecked or another dwindles, the entire ecosystem feels the impact. Yet, nature has an inherent corrective mechanism—a built-in resilience that seeks to restore equilibrium. Droughts, floods, natural predators, and resource scarcity serve as checks and balances, ensuring that no species overwhelms the system.

Nature's support, however, is not unconditional; it rewards adaptability. Those who adjust to changes in the environment survive and thrive, while rigidity often leads to extinction. Adaptability is not merely a passive trait but an active engagement with one's surroundings—an openness to learn, change, and evolve. The classic example is Darwin's observation of the finches in the Galápagos Islands. Each species of finch evolved a beak shape best suited to its specific food source. This adaptability ensured their survival amidst shifting environmental conditions. Similarly, the peppered moth in England changed color from light to dark during the Industrial Revolution to camouflage against soot-darkened trees, demonstrating rapid evolutionary response. Human beings, too, are subject to this law. Civilizations that adapted to changing climates, shifting resources, and evolving technologies flourished, while those that resisted change often perished. Adaptability thus emerges as the master key nature hands out to those willing to survive and thrive.

Closely tied to adaptability is adoptability—the willingness to accept and integrate new behaviors, ideas, and practices. Adaptability allows one to adjust to external changes; adoptability enables the internalization of new modes of existence. In nature, examples abound. Migratory birds change their nesting grounds based on climatic shifts. Trees in temperate zones shed their leaves to conserve water during winter, adopting dormancy as a strategy. Even microorganisms exhibit adoptability—bacteria can acquire resistance to antibiotics by integrating new genetic material.

For humans, adoptability becomes even more crucial in the modern age. Technological advancements, social transformations, and global interconnectivity demand that individuals not only adapt but also adopt new skills, mindsets, and behaviors. Those who resist learning and change often find themselves marginalized.

By consciously developing adaptability and adoptability, living beings, especially humans, can enhance both the quality and the span of their lives. Adaptability thrives on learning. Just as organisms in nature learn from their environments, humans benefit immensely from continuous education—not merely formal schooling but a lifelong commitment to acquiring new knowledge and skills. Resilience is the ability to bounce back from adversity. Nature's most enduring beings are those that recover from disruptions—the forest regenerating after a fire, the coral reefs rebuilding after bleaching events.

Humans, too, can cultivate resilience through mental flexibility, emotional intelligence, and a positive outlook. Rigid thinking and behavior are akin to a dry, brittle branch that breaks under pressure. Flexible minds and behaviors, like a reed that bends in the wind, withstand challenges. Embracing diverse perspectives, being open to feedback, and experimenting with new methods are hallmarks of flexibility.

Adaptability extends to physical health. The body's immune system, for instance, adapts to new pathogens. A lifestyle that incorporates adaptability—balanced diet, regular exercise, mindfulness practices—enhances vitality and longevity. In a world driven by rapid technological innovation and social change, adaptability and adoptability are indispensable. Those who integrate new technologies, adapt to new work cultures, and adopt sustainable practices position themselves for long-term success and relevance.

In the unforgiving Arctic environment, the fox survives by changing its coat color—brown in summer, white in winter—an adaptive feature that ensures camouflage and successful hunting. The banyan tree spreads its roots and branches widely, creating support pillars that allow it to sustain its massive structure. Its adoptability to various soil types and conditions enables it to thrive across different terrains. Neuroplasticity—the brain's ability to reorganize itself by forming new neural connections—is a remarkable example of adaptability. It allows humans to recover from injuries, learn new skills, and adjust to changing circumstances.

Despite nature's clear endorsement of adaptability and adoptability, barriers often arise, particularly among humans. Fear of Change: Change brings uncertainty, and fear often paralyzes initiative.

Attachment to Comfort: Familiarity breeds comfort, and the reluctance to step out of the comfort zone hinders growth. Ego and Inflexibility: A rigid ego resists feedback and alternative viewpoints, stalling evolution. Lack of Awareness: Many remain unaware of the need for adaptability until it is too late. Addressing these barriers involves cultivating a growth mindset—believing that abilities and intelligence can be developed—and embracing change as an opportunity rather than a threat.

Climate change, pandemics, technological disruption—the 21st century presents unprecedented challenges. Nature's lesson is more relevant than ever: those who adapt and adopt will endure and flourish. Cities are adopting green technologies; Industries are adapting to digital revolutions; Individuals are adopting remote work and virtual collaboration. Societies that resist these changes face decline, while those embracing them pave the way for sustainable, inclusive futures.

Nature's nurturing care extends an open invitation to all life forms—survive, grow, and thrive. Yet, this invitation comes with an unspoken expectation: adapt and adopt. By tuning into this natural rhythm, by observing and learning from nature's examples, individuals can vastly enhance their quality of life and extend their existence.

Life, at its best, is a continuous dialogue between the being and its environment. Those who listen, learn, and align with the eternal principles of adaptability and adoptability not only survive but create richer, fuller, and more meaningful lives. In doing so, they become not mere beneficiaries but conscious co-creators in the grand, unfolding symphony of nature. In the end, the choice lies with us: resist change and face extinction, or embrace adaptability and adoptability to dance in harmony with the universe. Nature, ever caring and patient, has already shown the way.

❐

Chapter-4

Improvement Demands Sincere Effort—This is the Lesson Nature Teaches Us Through the Law of Entropy

In the grand theatre of existence, every entity is inexorably tied to the laws of nature. From the origin of the cosmos to the delicate unfolding of a flower, from the movement of stars to the beating of a heart, all phenomena obey fundamental principles. Among these, the principle that disorder, or entropy, tends to increase in a closed system naturally and spontaneously unless energy is supplied from outside, holds profound implications not only in the realm of physics but also in the sphere of personal growth and personality development.

Nature operates on immutable laws. One such law, the second law of thermodynamics, states that within a closed system, the degree of disorder increases with time, naturally and spontaneously. Left to themselves, systems drift towards chaos. A well-ordered room will accumulate dust; a meticulously maintained garden will, without tending, become overgrown. The implication is clear: maintaining order, let alone improving it, requires the infusion of energy from external sources. This fundamental reality can be extended metaphorically to human personality and societal structures.

The human personality is, in many ways, a complex system — a web of thoughts, emotions, behaviors, and aspirations. Without conscious effort and directed energy, this system too will tend toward disorder. Habits deteriorate, motivation wanes, relationships erode, and clarity of purpose fades. Thus, maintaining the integrity of one's character demands constant nourishment and vigilant self-awareness.

Consider the mind as a closed system. If it is left unattended, it will not naturally incline toward higher states of discipline, creativity, or virtue. Instead, negativity, confusion, lethargy, and chaos are more likely to prevail. This tendency toward disorder is a silent process, often unnoticed until its effects become pronounced. To counteract this, energy must be supplied — in the form of learning, reflection, practice, and conscious action.

Learning is an active process that introduces new order into the mind. Each new idea, when critically examined and thoughtfully integrated, organizes mental chaos into a coherent structure of understanding. Reflection serves to align actions with values, and practice engrains desirable habits. These acts of directed energy maintain the mind's equilibrium and can even improve its order, elevating the individual toward greater wisdom and effectiveness.

Physical health too follows a similar trajectory. The body, if neglected, succumbs to the entropy of disease, weakness, and decay. Sustaining health requires the infusion of external energy: nourishment through food, vitality through exercise, and resilience through rest and recovery. Merely existing is insufficient; active and intelligent effort is necessary to maintain and enhance the physical vessel that houses our being.

In relationships, entropy manifests as the gradual breakdown of understanding, trust, and affection if not consciously maintained. Emotional connections require the energy of communication, empathy, compromise, and shared experiences. Left unattended, even the strongest bonds can wither under the entropy of neglect.

Society at large reflects the same principle. Civilizations decline when the energy of innovation, ethical governance, and cultural refinement wanes. Social systems, without active nurturing, devolve into disorder and dysfunction. It is the responsibility of each individual to contribute their energy to the collective, ensuring that order and progress are sustained.

Returning to nature, we find that it too resists entropy through the constant influx of energy from the sun. Plants capture solar energy through photosynthesis, forming the basis of life's intricate web. Without this continuous supply of energy, the delicate balance of ecosystems would collapse into chaos. In the grand design, survival and flourishing depend on the capacity to capture, store, and effectively utilize energy.

In the realm of personality development, this means that passive existence cannot suffice. Life demands active engagement. To maintain our values, disciplines, and aspirations, we must consistently draw energy from sources of inspiration, knowledge, and practice. To grow — to elevate our consciousness, refine our character, and realize our potential — demands an even greater investment of energy.

Self-discipline is one such vital infusion of energy. It is the ongoing, conscious effort to align one's actions with chosen principles. Without discipline, the mind and body revert to their default state of inertia and impulsivity. Discipline supplies the steady energy required to resist immediate gratification in favor of long-term fulfillment.

Another indispensable energy source is purpose. A clearly defined sense of purpose acts as a guiding star, organizing one's life toward meaningful ends. It energizes action, focuses attention, and fortifies resilience. Purpose transforms scattered efforts into coherent, directed endeavors, reducing internal disorder and amplifying personal power.

Mindfulness, the art of present-moment awareness, acts as a stabilizing force against the entropy of distraction and mindlessness. By being fully present, we prevent the mind from drifting into chaos. Mindfulness, cultivated through practices like meditation and conscious breathing, supplies the calming energy needed to maintain mental clarity and emotional balance.

Creativity too is an antidote to disorder. It reorganizes existing elements into novel, harmonious forms. Engaging in creative pursuits introduces a dynamic vitality into life, combating the stagnation and decay that unchallenged routines bring.

Importantly, the supply of energy must be intelligent and harmonious with the system's needs. Blind exertion or haphazard effort can create more chaos rather than resolve it. Thus, wisdom must guide energy's application, ensuring that effort aligns with purpose and that action is informed by understanding.

Equally crucial is the recognition that energy resources are finite. Human beings have limited reservoirs of physical, mental, and emotional energy. Therefore, the principle of conservation must be employed. Energy should not be squandered on trivial pursuits, unworthy conflicts, or mindless distractions. Strategic focus — choosing where and how to direct one's energy — becomes paramount.

This notion leads us to the importance of rest and rejuvenation. Just as systems cannot be sustained by constant energy expenditure without periods of recovery, so too the human organism requires cycles of exertion and renewal. Sleep, leisure, silence, and introspection are not luxuries; they are essential components of a sustainable life. They restore depleted energies and prepare the individual for renewed engagement with life's demands.

Furthermore, emotional and moral energies must be cultivated. Compassion, gratitude, patience, and humility are energies that stabilize and uplift the personality. They counteract the entropic forces of anger, greed, envy, and pride. Moral virtues are not inherent; they must be consciously cultivated, practiced, and replenished.

The broader implication of this principle is that personality development is not a one-time achievement but a lifelong endeavor. There is no permanent plateau where one can rest indefinitely. The forces of entropy are relentless, and vigilance is essential. Continuous learning, self-assessment, and renewal are non-negotiable.

Personal entropy also challenges us to recognize the interconnectedness of all life. Just as individual systems require external energy, we too depend on the energies of others: love, friendship, inspiration, and collaboration. No man is an island, and the energies that sustain us often come through the channels of community and shared human experience.

Ultimately, the natural law that disorder increases unless energy is supplied reminds us of life's precious fragility and the immense responsibility we bear for our own growth. To maintain order within ourselves, and to elevate it, we must be diligent gardeners of our inner landscapes, constantly supplying the needed energy, pruning the overgrowth of distractions, watering the roots of purpose, and exposing ourselves to the sunlight of knowledge and virtue.

In every moment of choice, we either supply energy to sustain and enhance order, or we permit the silent encroachment of disorder. The quality of our lives, the strength of our character, and the legacy we leave behind depend on this continual dance with entropy.

Nature teaches us that decay is inevitable without effort, that flourishing is a reward reserved for those who labor wisely and persistently. The universe, in its quiet majesty, offers no exemptions to this law. It falls upon us to heed its message, to respect its wisdom, and to live in harmony with its truth.

Thus, personality development is not merely an aspiration but a necessity dictated by the very fabric of reality. To live well, to grow, and to leave the world better than we found it, we must supply the energy that order demands. In this endeavor, nature is not only our mirror but also our mentor.

The silent wisdom of the cosmos awaits those who are willing to listen, learn, and labor.

"In all things of nature, there is something of the marvelous."

— Aristotle

❒

Chapter-5

In Nature, creation is silent and smooth—jerks or noise signal destruction

In the profound theater of life, where forces visible and invisible shape the world, a quiet truth governs the rhythm of existence: construction — whether of a being, a relationship, a civilization, or a universe — is invariably silent, smooth, and spontaneous. In contrast, sudden jerks, loud disruptions, and violent sounds herald destruction. Across nature, history, and the inner realms of the human soul, this silent law repeats itself with unwavering fidelity. Those who understand it gain a glimpse into the delicate mechanics of creation and the ferocious mechanics of dissolution.

In nature, construction is the work of patience and subtlety. Observe a seed transforming into a towering tree. Day after day, quietly and invisibly, roots anchor themselves in the earth, shoots push towards the light, leaves unfurl. There is no grand sound, no sudden eruption, no fanfare. The growth is smooth, rhythmic, almost imperceptible. Yet, year after year, the silent labor of life constructs forests, green sanctuaries where life flourishes.

Contrast this with the destruction of that same forest — a wildfire sparked in an instant, roaring, crackling, consuming in a matter of hours what took centuries to grow. The difference is not merely one of outcome but of process. Construction respects the rhythm of time, the discipline of gradualism, the elegance of silence. Destruction, on the other hand, disrespects time, erupts violently, and announces itself with noise and suddenness.

This principle is not confined to trees and forests. It extends to the growth of mountains, the formation of rivers, the weaving of ecosystems. Mountains rise over millennia, as tectonic plates shift slowly, almost imperceptibly. Rivers carve canyons over eons, not with sudden floods but with the patient caress of water on stone. The intricate web of an ecosystem — the balance of predator and prey, the dance of pollinators and plants — emerges through countless small adjustments, quiet adaptations, silent negotiations.

Destruction, when it comes, shatters this subtle harmony. A volcanic eruption, an earthquake, a hurricane — all are abrupt, loud, and devastating. The constructive forces of nature work silently and seamlessly, building complexity and order without disturbance; destructive forces tear it apart noisily and swiftly.

In the human body, too, construction is a silent symphony. The growth of a child from embryo to adult is a marvel of silent, continuous construction. Cells divide, organs form, bones lengthen, muscles strengthen — all without any grand display. Health, vitality, and strength are built quietly through balanced nutrition, rest, and gentle effort.

When destruction occurs — disease, injury, decay — it often announces itself with pain, swelling, fever, and dysfunction. These are the body's alarms, signals that the smooth process of construction has been disrupted. Healing, when it happens, resumes the original quiet rhythm — the body repairs wounds, knits bones, and mends tissues silently and patiently.

Extend this observation to the human mind and soul. The construction of character, wisdom, and virtue is not an overnight achievement. It is the result of silent reflections, daily disciplines, small acts of courage, kindness, and honesty. No thunder accompanies the growth of patience or the cultivation of humility. The true building of a strong and serene personality is an inward, unpublicized affair, a series of quiet victories over anger, greed, fear, and pride.

Yet destruction of character can be swift and noisy. A single act of betrayal, a burst of uncontrolled rage, a sudden fall into temptation — these can undo years of quiet construction. Loud arguments, dramatic breakdowns, impulsive actions — all are symptoms not of construction but of destruction.

The same principle applies to relationships. Strong, enduring relationships — whether friendships, partnerships, or marriages — are built in silence, through trust, respect, and consistent affection. There are no fireworks when trust is built, no grand proclamations when loyalty is cemented. It is in the quiet sharing of burdens, the unnoticed acts of care, the spontaneous kindnesses that relationships are forged.

When relationships falter, the signs are loud and sudden: heated arguments, harsh words, abrupt departures. Trust, built silently over years, can be shattered in seconds by a sudden betrayal. Love, nourished quietly, can be destroyed by loud accusations and impulsive acts. Where there is noise, violence, and sudden jerks, there is destruction.

Civilizations themselves are governed by this law. The construction of a civilization — its culture, institutions, knowledge, and values — is a slow, cumulative process. Great civilizations emerge over centuries, not overnight. They are the products of countless minds thinking, building, writing, debating — often in obscurity, often without recognition. Libraries are filled, philosophies refined, laws codified — all through a patient, often silent labor.

Destruction of civilizations, however, is often abrupt and loud. Wars, invasions, revolutions — these bring about rapid downfall. The sacking of Rome, the fall of Constantinople, the collapse of the Mayan civilization — all were accompanied by violence and noise, sweeping away centuries of slow, quiet construction in a matter of months or years.

Even in human endeavors — business, art, science — true construction follows the quiet, smooth, and spontaneous path. An artist's masterpiece is not the product of a sudden burst but of years of silent practice, countless drafts, and disciplined creativity. A scientist's discovery is not the result of one thunderous revelation but of painstaking experiments, repeated failures, and patient analysis. A great company is not built in the frenzy of one successful product launch but in years of quiet work: hiring carefully, building trust with customers, refining processes.

Destruction in these fields, however, is quick and noisy. A business collapses due to sudden scandals or reckless decisions. A reputation built over decades can be destroyed in a moment of indiscretion. The principle holds unfailingly: creation is slow, silent, and smooth; destruction is sudden, loud, and violent.

The very universe follows this rhythm. Stars are born from the silent gathering of dust and gas over millions of years. Galaxies form from the gradual coalescence of matter. Life itself emerged through a slow, steady process of evolution, unfolding across eons. Yet, when stars die, they explode in supernovae — bright, violent, and sudden. Planets can be destroyed by collisions in an instant. Entire galaxies can be ripped apart by cosmic forces in violent upheavals.

This deep principle is mirrored in our inner lives as well. Spiritual growth — the construction of a deep inner peace, a robust inner joy, a resilient soul — is a silent process. It is cultivated in solitude, in meditation, in the slow transformation of thought and habit. There are no sudden revelations that can substitute for the steady accumulation of insight, compassion, and wisdom.

Spiritual destruction, however, can be sudden. A mind consumed by hatred, greed, or fear can collapse into despair or violence. Peace, built over years, can be shattered by a single uncontrolled emotion. Thus, the silent, smooth, spontaneous path of construction must be guarded carefully against the sudden, noisy impulses that herald destruction.

Understanding this law is essential for wise living. It teaches patience — for anything truly worthwhile must be constructed slowly and silently. It teaches vigilance — for sudden disruptions often presage downfall. It teaches humility — for the grandeur of construction lies not in public applause but in quiet perseverance. It teaches reverence — for all that is truly beautiful, lasting, and meaningful is built in silence and can be destroyed in an instant.

In daily life, this understanding can transform our approach to goals, relationships, learning, and personal growth. It cautions against impatience — against the desire for quick results, instant gratification, immediate recognition. It encourages the cultivation of habits that may seem small but, over time, build great strength. It invites us to trust the silent processes — the learning that happens beneath awareness, the healing that occurs without drama, the growth that is invisible but inexorable.

It also alerts us to the dangers of noise — not merely literal noise but the noise of distractions, of unregulated emotions, of impulsive actions. It warns against the seductions of drama, the lure of shortcuts, the intoxication of rapid success without foundation. It calls for a life lived in quiet discipline, in smooth continuity, in spontaneous flow, trusting that true construction needs no loud announcement but reveals itself in time.

Moreover, it offers solace in times of frustration. When progress seems invisible, when growth feels too slow, when success appears distant, remembering that true construction is silent reassures us. It reminds us that the most profound changes often occur unnoticed, that the deepest roots grow underground, that the most enduring structures are built stone by stone, quietly, patiently.

History honors the builders — those who labored quietly for years before their work was recognized. The great cathedrals of Europe, some of which took centuries to complete, were built by generations of artisans who knew they would not live to see the final result. They worked not for fame but for the joy of construction itself. Scientists like Newton and Darwin spent decades in quiet study before presenting theories that changed the world. Artists like Van Gogh painted in obscurity, quietly creating works that would only be celebrated after their deaths. Their lives affirm that construction is not for the impatient, the loud, or the impulsive. It is for the quiet, the patient, the steadfast.

Even revolutions, when they succeed in creating lasting good, are not merely the result of a sudden uprising but of long, silent periods of preparation — of ideas incubated, of movements built patiently, of minds educated quietly. The loud explosion is often only the visible tip of an iceberg of silent, slow construction.

In the final analysis, life itself is a testament to this principle. The heart beats quietly, the breath flows softly, the cells regenerate invisibly. Our very existence is sustained by countless silent processes. When sudden jerks occur — a heart attack, a stroke — they disrupt life. Health is silent construction; disease is noisy destruction.

Thus, from the smallest cell to the grandest civilization, from the growth of a single tree to the birth of galaxies, the lesson is clear: construction is always silent, smooth, and spontaneous. It unfolds patiently, without fanfare, without sudden leaps. When there are sudden jerks or loud disruptions, when there is noise and violence, there is not construction but destruction.

To live wisely is to align with this eternal law — to build patiently, to grow quietly, to trust the silent rhythms of life. It is to respect the slow processes that nurture true strength, to guard against the sudden impulses that invite ruin, to find joy not in the noise of applause but in the silent satisfaction of creation.

Life rewards those who understand and honor this law. For they build not just structures or achievements but character, peace, and wisdom — foundations that endure beyond the reach of time and turbulence.

❐

Chapter-6
Work itself generates its result—Nature teaches us this through the law of cause and effect

The universe, in all its vastness and complexity, may seem random at first glance. Storms rage, stars explode, people succeed or fail, and events unfold with a bewildering unpredictability. Yet beneath this apparent chaos lies an eternal and unchanging principle—the law of cause and effect. Every event, every phenomenon, every action springs from a cause. Nothing in existence occurs without reason.

This principle is not confined merely to the physical world; it extends into the realms of morality, psychology, social systems, and spiritual evolution. Known in Sanskrit as *Karya-Karana Niyama*, the law of cause and effect is a foundation upon which Indian philosophical systems such as Vedanta, Sankhya, and Buddhism have built their profound insights. Modern science, too, rests upon this law. Popular wisdom distills it into the simple but powerful phrase: *As you sow, so shall you reap.*

In the physical sciences, the law of cause-and-effect reigns supreme. Newton's third law—that for every action, there is an equal and opposite reaction—is a reflection of this universal principle. Disciplines like physics, chemistry, and biology operate on the assumption that specific results follow specific causes. Water forms only when hydrogen and oxygen combine in precise proportions under particular conditions. Genetic inheritance determines the traits passed from parents to offspring. Earthquakes arise because of tectonic movements beneath the Earth's crust. In every corner of nature, effects arise not by chance but by necessity, dictated by preceding causes.

Even chaos theory, which studies complex and seemingly unpredictable systems, does not deny causality; rather, it reveals that the universe is sensitive to initial conditions. Small causes can lead to disproportionately large effects—a phenomenon popularly known as the butterfly effect, where the flap of a butterfly's wings in Brazil might ultimately trigger a tornado in Texas. It is not randomness but an intricate responsiveness that governs the unfolding of events.

Human psychology operates no differently. Every thought, every emotion, every behavior can be traced back to causes—whether external stimuli, internal choices, or deep-seated mental impressions known as *samskaras*. Anxiety does not arise from a vacuum; it often stems from past trauma, present stress, or fear of the future. Anger erupts from perceived injustice; love blossoms from empathy, care, and connection. Success is not mere luck but the cumulative result of sustained effort, clear purpose, skill, and discipline.

Thoughts, seemingly ephemeral, are potent causes. They give rise to actions; actions repeated become habits; habits, in turn, weave the fabric of character. This is why spiritual traditions place profound emphasis on cultivating right thinking, for in the subtle movements of thought lies the blueprint of destiny. The Buddha expressed it succinctly: *"All that we are is the result of what we have thought. The mind is everything. What we think, we become."* Thus, the invisible movements of the mind ripple outward, shaping emotions, behaviors, and the courses of our lives.

Nowhere does the law of cause and effect find deeper moral integration than in the doctrine of karma. Karma, meaning action, implies that every deed—physical, verbal, or mental—carries consequences. Acts of kindness sow seeds of joy; acts of cruelty sow seeds of suffering. These consequences are not the products of divine favor or wrath but are the impartial outcomes of the natural moral law that governs the universe as surely as gravity governs the physical world. Poison seeds do not grow into mango trees; selfishness does not bear peace as its fruit.

The diversity of human experience—one born into affluence, another into hardship; one enjoying robust health, another plagued by illness—finds explanation in the invisible ledger of karmic causality. Some causes are visible, unfolding within the span of a lifetime; others are hidden, stretching back into the mists of previous existences. Yet karma should not be mistaken for fatalism. It does not suggest that the future is fixed and immutable. Just as the seeds sown yesterday bear today's fruit, the seeds sown today will shape tomorrow's harvest. Karma, therefore, is not a chain but a key—an empowering principle that places the shaping of the future in the hands of present action and intention.

The law of cause and effect extends far beyond individuals; it envelops nations, societies, and civilizations. A corrupt system is not immune to consequence; in time, it collapses under the weight of its own decay. A society that suppresses truth eventually drowns in the chaos of its own lies. A civilization that exploits nature will, without fail, face environmental devastation.

History stands as a silent witness to this unyielding law. Rome, the grand empire, fell not simply due to external invasion, but because of internal moral decay. Nazi Germany was consumed by the violence it unleashed upon the world. Civil rights movements emerged as inevitable reactions to long-standing oppression. Every social structure, every societal condition, is an effect born from causes set in motion long before the effect manifests. Injustice ignored today becomes the rebellion of tomorrow.

Conversely, societies that plant the seeds of education, justice, equality, and ethics flourish. Japan, rising from the ashes of devastation, rebuilt itself through discipline, unity, and an unyielding commitment to progress. South Korea, once impoverished, transformed into an economic powerhouse through a deliberate investment in technological education and hard work. The effects are visible to all who care to see—the undeniable fruits of carefully cultivated causes.

In the realm of spirituality, the law of cause and effect maps the journey toward liberation. Human bondage is not the result of external curses or original sins but is caused by ignorance, ego, selfish desires, and attachment. When these causes are removed, the corresponding effect—suffering—dissolves. Vedanta teaches that misidentification with the transient body and restless mind is the fundamental cause of human suffering. When a person realizes the eternal truth of the Self, the Atman, the false causes of fear, anger, and sorrow evaporate.

Buddhism, in its profound analysis, presents the Twelve Nidanas, the chain of dependent origination, to explain how suffering arises. Ignorance leads to mental formations, which lead to consciousness, and the chain continues, inevitably birthing suffering. Liberation, then, lies not in supernatural intervention but in the precise and methodical removal of these causes. It is a scientific, causal unfolding: transform the causes, and the effects are transformed. Sow mindfulness, compassion, detachment, and wisdom, and one will inevitably harvest freedom.

An understanding of the law of cause and effect is not reserved for philosophers and sages alone; it can transform daily life. It teaches responsibility, mindfulness, emotional maturity, vision, patience, and perseverance. To grasp responsibility is to recognize that life is not an accident.

Your present conditions are the result of causes—some of your making, some inherited. Instead of cursing fate, the wise ask: "What did I do—or fail to do—that brought me here?" Such inquiry empowers. Every thought, word, and deed is a seed sown into the fabric of reality. Before acting, consider: What effect will this cause? Impure causes cannot yield pure effects; recognizing this sharpens moral clarity.

Emotional maturity grows when we understand that those who hurt us are often acting from their own pain, fear, or ignorance. This awareness breeds compassion and reduces reactive anger. With this vision, the future becomes malleable. If you desire peace, cultivate understanding. If you seek success, sow discipline. If you yearn for love, plant seeds of kindness. The future is not a mystery; it is the delayed echo of the present moment.

Patience and faith are necessary companions on this path. Causes, like seeds, require time to bear fruit. A farmer does not abandon the field because the sprout is slow to emerge; so too must we trust the invisible workings of cause and effect. Good actions may not produce immediate visible results, but they are never lost.

Despite its universal truth, the law of cause and effect is often misunderstood. Delayed effects and hidden causes make people doubt. It seems unjust that an immoral person may thrive while a virtuous one suffers. But appearances deceive. Just as a mango seed takes years to bear fruit, karmic results often unfold over long, unseen timelines. According to Hindu and Buddhist traditions, these timelines can stretch across lifetimes. Furthermore, life is complex, and multiple causes often converge to produce a single effect. Illness, for example, may arise from a tangle of genetic, dietary, environmental, and emotional causes. Understanding causality, therefore, demands patience, reflection, and depth of insight.

Analogies help illuminate this principle. Life is like a garden; every action is a seed. If you plant roses, you will not harvest *acacia arabica* (babool). But neglect the weeds, and they will overrun the blossoms. Good actions must be nourished, bad habits uprooted. Life is also like an echo—what you project into the valley returns to you. Shout anger, and anger reverberates back. Whisper love, and love responds. The universe mirrors back the energy we release. Or think of a boomerang—whatever you send out, in thoughts, words, or deeds, will circle back to you. Harm returns harm; help returns help.

The law of cause and effect is not merely an abstract idea; it is the invisible thread that holds the universe together. It ensures that existence is not a chaotic theater, but a meaningful arena governed by justice and evolution. From the steady orbits of planets to the delicate unfolding of a flower, from the rise and fall of empires to the individual joys and sorrows that shape human lives—all obey this law. Aligning with it, we cease to be mere spectators and become conscious co-creators of our destiny. Life no longer appears as a game of luck or injustice but becomes a canvas where the brushstrokes of our choices and efforts paint the future.

As Mahatma Gandhi once observed, *"The law of karma is inexorable; it knows no forgiveness. It is the law of cause and effect. We reap what we sow."* In this truth lies a profound paradox: warning and hope intertwined. If we do not like the harvest, we have the power to change the seeds we plant. The law of cause and effect is not a chain binding us to a fixed fate—it is a key, offering the possibility of freedom.

❒

Chapter-7

It is not the action, but the intention behind it that defines its value

In the vast theatre of life, every moment hums with action—people speak, work, build, teach, protest, donate, punish, heal, and create. On the surface, all these acts seem equally valid. But look deeper, and the curtain lifts on a more profound truth: it is not merely the action, but the intention behind it that gives an act its true moral and spiritual weight. A businessman donating to charity, a judge sentencing a criminal, a soldier pulling a trigger, a teacher scolding a child—all these may appear as ordinary or dramatic gestures. But the soul of each act lies not in its form, but in its motive. In simple yet transformative terms: **intention is more important than the work**.

This truth echoes through the heart of every spiritual tradition, philosophical doctrine, and moral code ever known. It is the foundation of karma, the pulse of ethics, the breath of character. A grand act done for selfish gain carries no sanctity. Yet even a humble deed, when born of love and sincerity, radiates immeasurable moral power.

Actions are like trees—what the world sees is the fruit. But the fruit's sweetness or poison lies in the health of its root. The root is the intention, unseen yet decisive. A shiny apple grown from poisoned soil is dangerous; similarly, a beautiful-looking act rooted in selfishness is ultimately corrupt. The intention, though invisible, determines the essence and outcome of every action. It either nourishes or poisons the deed.

Indian philosophy, particularly its understanding of karma, affirms this timeless principle. It is not merely what one does, but why one does it that holds lasting value. The Bhagavad Gita sings this truth again and again, most famously when Krishna says to Arjuna, *"Karmanye vadhikaraste, ma phaleshu kadachana"*—you are entitled to your actions, but never to the fruits of those actions. Why this insistence? Because only intention is truly within our grasp.

The outcome is shaped by many forces—circumstances, time, others' choices—but the intention arises purely from the self.

A surgeon may act with total sincerity and still lose the patient. A teacher may pour heart and soul into a student who still fails. Should they be called failures? Never. Because their actions, regardless of outcome, were grounded in integrity. On the other hand, if one acts from greed, anger, pride, or selfish ambition—even if the visible result appears useful—the act carries an invisible corruption. That is the silent rot in the fruit. The true karma, in such cases, is tainted. In the divine ledger, it is the purity of the heart, not the glitter of the result, that counts.

Even secular systems like criminal justice recognize this. The same physical act—causing a death—can be judged as murder or as accident depending on the intention. Religions affirm this too. Jesus in Christianity elevated the inner spirit of the law above its outward observance. In Buddhism, "right intention" is one of the eight central paths to liberation. Jainism and Hinduism, too, speak of *ahimsa* not merely as physical non-violence but as a purity of heart. Morality, in every tradition, is rooted not in hands but in hearts.

Psychologically too, intentions form the bedrock of personality. Actions may be manipulated or mechanical. Intentions reveal the soul. They are conscious choices, mirrors of the will. A person who says sorry just to escape blame is not sincere. A person who helps out of guilt may still be carrying an unresolved burden. A student who studies with genuine curiosity will grow, while one who memorizes for marks will merely pass time. It is the reason behind the effort that shapes the inner self. Intentions build character, and character builds destiny.

From the spiritual lens, this becomes even more refined. Saints and sages have long taught that spiritual growth lies not in quantity but in quality—not in ritual but in *bhava*, the felt intention behind a prayer, a service, or an offering. One heartfelt tear can outweigh a thousand rote chants. Saint Kabir cautioned that we should live in such a way that people mourn our loss, not for what we did outwardly, but for the love and service with which we did it. Krishna, in the Gita, accepts even a leaf or a drop of water—if offered with devotion. It is not the size of the offering, but the love behind it that pleases the Divine.

Yet in this achievement-driven world, people often forget this. Society celebrates success, results, power, and appearances. Few pause to ask: at what cost was this done? With what intention? This blindness leads to a distortion of values. The outward deed is praised; the inner motive ignored. But history sees more clearly. It does not just remember what was done—but why. Gandhi is remembered not just for leading India's freedom struggle, but for the moral purpose behind it. His truth and non-violence were intentions, not just strategies. Mother Teresa didn't build institutions; she offered compassion. Her power lay in the purity of her motive. It is such intention that turns ordinary work into eternal work.

If one wishes to purify intention, the path is clear though not always easy. Ask yourself honestly: Why am I doing this? Is it to help, to be praised, to manipulate, or to contribute sincerely? Detach from obsession with results—work sincerely, and release the rest. Intention matures when selfishness is seen and shed. Be truthful with yourself, without wearing masks. Pretending to be selfless blocks growth. Gratitude also purifies motive. When we act with a thankful heart, we give more than we demand. Silence, meditation, and prayer align us with our deeper self—where intention can rise free of ego and distortion.

Even in the fast-paced world of professions and ambition, intention remains the hidden key to greatness. A teacher who teaches to ignite minds makes an everlasting impact. A doctor who heals with compassion becomes more than a technician—they become a channel of grace. A leader who governs with justice, not ego, earns lasting trust. When institutions are driven by sincere intent—by truth, service, and collective good—they become vehicles of transformation. But when driven by vanity, competition, and manipulation, they eventually collapse.

And in the smallest of acts, intention still reigns. No one may see your silent forgiveness. No one may hear your whispered prayer. But these acts shape your soul. In a world obsessed with noise, silent and pure intentions are the quiet architects of change. They are seeds of compassion, planted deep, blooming when least expected.

Work matters. Action is essential. But without the fire of pure intention, action is a body without soul, a structure without foundation. Intention is the subtle light behind the visible flame. It decides whether our actions build or destroy, bless or burden, elevate or imprison. In a world that constantly asks, “What are you doing?”—let us have the courage to ask instead, “Why are you doing it?”

Let us live not just to act, but to act from the heart.

Not just to succeed, but to serve.

Not just to perform, but to purify.

For in the end, it is not the size of our work, but the sincerity of our purpose that reveals who we truly are.

❐

Chapter-8
Nature teaches that mutuality is the root of growth—the law of give and take in action

From the gentle flow of rivers that give water to the fields, to the unspoken contract between bees and flowers, the entire cosmos operates on one fundamental law: the law of give and take. Whether in nature, human relationships, economics, spirituality, or morality, nothing exists in isolation. Every entity—living or non-living—is interconnected through a web of mutual dependence and reciprocal exchange. This principle, often referred to as the law of reciprocity or balance, is not only practical but also deeply moral, spiritual, and universal in its application.

Throughout the natural world, the beauty of this principle unfolds in countless ways. The earth provides oxygen, water, food, and shelter, yet always within a greater cycle of exchange. Plants absorb carbon dioxide and release oxygen, while animals and humans exhale carbon dioxide, completing the loop. Should this delicate balance be disturbed—by, for instance, excessive carbon emissions—the planet responds, not with punishment, but by restoring equilibrium, reminding us that taking without giving is unsustainable.

The mutual relationships among living organisms embody this law vividly: lichens, formed by fungi and algae, exchange protection and food; bees pollinate flowers while gathering nectar; forests contribute moisture to the atmosphere, and the rains nourish them in return. Even death is woven into this sacred balance—fallen leaves and decaying creatures fertilize the soil, enabling new life to emerge. Nature wastes nothing; everything borrowed is eventually returned in another form. When humanity disregards this rhythm—through overconsumption, deforestation, or pollution—disasters inevitably follow. Nature does not punish; it simply and silently resets the balance.

In the human sphere, this law underpins all relationships. Trust, affection, and respect are not one-way gifts; they flourish only when there is mutual giving and receiving. In marriage, for example, both partners must invest time, energy, and care to sustain the relationship. When one gives constantly while the other merely takes, imbalance ensues and resentment festers. Friendships thrive on mutual support and empathy, and even the bond between parent and child reflects this pattern—children who receive love and guidance eventually give back through gratitude, affection, and their contributions to society.

The same pattern extends to larger human communities. A society that demands obedience but withholds justice, security, and dignity will eventually decay. Likewise, citizens who claim rights without fulfilling responsibilities weaken the very fabric of their nation. Stability, both social and political, depends on a continuous and reciprocal exchange of duties and entitlements.

Economics, at its core, operates on the law of give and take. Money serves as a medium for the exchange of goods and services; labor is exchanged for wages; products are exchanged for payment. Taxes, though often resented, represent a contribution by citizens toward collective goods—law, infrastructure, education, and health—that in turn benefit the contributors. Across economic systems—capitalism, socialism, barter, even gift economies—the underlying principle remains constant: value must be given to receive value in return.

When this balance is violated, whether through exploitation or the pursuit of profit without corresponding value creation, instability and unrest soon follow. Debt and loans are clear examples: what is taken today must be returned tomorrow. Even acts of charity, though seemingly unconditional, imply a moral expectation: the hope that today's recipient may one day become tomorrow's giver.

Across civilizations, the progress of cultures has depended on this same principle of reciprocal exchange. No society has evolved in isolation. Ancient India gave the world the concept of zero and profound spiritual philosophies, and in turn absorbed architectural styles, agricultural knowledge, and philosophical ideas from other cultures. Greek thought influenced Roman governance, and the Roman legacy shaped modern European democracies.

Migration offers another vivid illustration: immigrants bring labor, diversity, and innovation; in return, they seek safety, opportunity, and dignity. Societies that welcome immigrants yet exploit them or deny them respect violate this delicate balance and sow seeds of conflict. Languages themselves bear witness to centuries of give and take. Hindi carries within it the echoes of Persian, Arabic, and English, just as English has absorbed words from Sanskrit, Latin, French, and German. In cuisine, music, art, and fashion, the richness of human creativity has been nourished by a continual, dynamic exchange of ideas and inspirations.

Thus, from the smallest organism to the grandest human achievements, from the unseen cycles of nature to the visible structures of civilization, the law of give and take threads its way through all existence, binding life together with silent, unbreakable ties. The more closely we observe, the more clearly we see: survival, growth, harmony, and evolution are all possible because of this timeless, universal principle.

All major spiritual traditions uphold the law of reciprocity as a sacred duty. In Hinduism, the concept of Yajna, the act of sacrifice or offering, embodies the belief that life itself is a divine exchange. One receives abundantly from nature, ancestors, gods, and society, and is thus morally bound to give back—through acts of service, charity, and self-restraint. The Bhagavad Gita captures this beautifully in its declaration that the gods, nourished by sacrifice, grant blessings in return. Christianity echoes this principle in the teaching: *"Do unto others as you would have them do unto you,"* a profound call to reciprocal compassion. Islam emphasizes Zakat, mandating the giving of a portion of one's wealth to support those in need. Buddhism places Dana, or generosity, at the very foundation of the path to enlightenment.

In each tradition, giving is not perceived as loss but as purification; taking without offering something back is seen as a spiritual imbalance, a theft from the larger harmony of life. Saints and mystics like Kabir, Nanak, and Rumi, across ages and cultures, have urged humanity to embrace giving—not merely of material possessions but of love, forgiveness, time, and wisdom.

Even within the inner chambers of the human heart and mind, the law of give and take governs well-being. The mind gives attention and is rewarded with knowledge. The heart pours out love and, in return, experiences joy. The soul offers silence and attains peace. Whenever this exchange falters, when one seeks only to receive—praise, attention, pleasure—without giving in return, dissatisfaction and inner emptiness creep in. Psychological health, like all else, depends on balance. Suppressed emotions breed tension; rest denied results in exhaustion. Releasing grudges creates emotional space for serenity.

Every step in personal growth follows this exchange—sacrificing laziness earns discipline; abandoning falsehood brings clarity; surrendering the ego fosters wisdom. Even the practice of counseling and therapy reflects this principle: the therapist extends listening and guidance, while the client, in turn, must offer honesty and effort for true transformation to take root.

Whenever this law of give and take is violated, the disturbance is inevitable. In nature, environmental destruction follows when humans extract resources without renewal—forests vanish, species perish, and climates grow increasingly hostile. Social inequality festers when power, privilege, and wealth are hoarded without redistribution. Emotional burnout consumes individuals when relationships are sustained by one-sided giving, devoid of care or recognition.

Economies falter when debt surpasses production or when profits are chased without genuine value creation. Even spiritual stagnation arises when individuals pray and plead for blessings yet fail to live ethically, to serve others, or to express gratitude. Though the collapse may not be immediate, the law reasserts itself with unyielding force. It is not a suggestion or an ideal—it is a cosmic necessity.

And yet, while taking is necessary for survival, it is giving that elevates life. It is giving that transforms base instinct into civilization, self-preservation into love, mere existence into profound meaning. When knowledge is shared, it breeds innovation and collective growth; when farmers share seeds, harvests multiply. Giving does not diminish—it enriches.

Societies founded on trust, cooperation, and shared responsibility flourish. Nations that invest in education and welfare produce not only prosperous economies but also responsible, engaged citizens. Giving, too, heals the giver. Studies affirm that individuals who volunteer, who help others, experience greater happiness and lower stress, discovering a purpose beyond self-interest.

Giving is liberation. It frees us from the chains of greed, fear, and attachment. As the ancient wisdom of the Upanishads proclaims, immortality is attained not through hoarding but through renunciation—through giving.

The law of give and take is not an abstract philosophy for saints or sages alone; it is the very foundation upon which survival, growth, and joy are built. Whether or not one believes in a divine power, this law silently governs every sphere of existence. When we receive knowledge, we are duty-bound to return it through teaching or meaningful application. When we are blessed with love, we must respond with gratitude and presence. When wealth finds its way into our lives, it must flow outward toward those less fortunate. When we draw from nature's bounty, we must replenish and protect it.

Life is not merely a transaction of currency; it is a sacred exchange of energies, values, time, and truth. To live well is to give where we can, take only what we need, and safeguard the balance that sustains all. In the end, it is not what we accumulate that measures the worth of our lives, but what we circulate—the love, wisdom, kindness, and service that we set flowing into the world. The world is not a stagnant storehouse; it is a living, breathing stream. Only those who move with its current—giving and receiving in harmony—find true peace and enduring purpose.

❐

Chapter-9

For as long as you are fit to adapt to your surroundings, you can grow and evolve

In the vast theater of life, nature unfolds its lessons quietly, impartially, and ceaselessly. Growth—the upward and outward journey of life—is a privilege not granted by mere existence but by fitness: the ability to adapt, endure, and flourish amidst changing conditions. In nature, the fit not only survive; they grow, thrive, and evolve.

For human beings, this truth has profound implications. Beyond mere survival, the capacity to grow physically, mentally, emotionally, and spiritually in harmony with nature is the mark of a truly fit person. Fitness here transcends the narrow confines of muscle strength or speed; it encompasses a holistic adaptability and resilience that embraces life in its fullest forms.

Fitness, when understood in human terms, extends far beyond physical prowess. While a strong and agile body remains important, true human fitness involves a synergy of physical endurance, mental sharpness, emotional resilience, and spiritual depth. A fit person has a body that can endure physical hardships like hunger, cold, and fatigue; a mind that can solve problems creatively and logically; emotions that foster cooperation, patience, and optimism; and a spirit that finds meaning even in suffering and change. It is this integrated fitness that enables humans not only to live in nature but to grow within it.

Growth in nature is not linear; it is dynamic, adaptive, and responsive to the environment. A tree grows where there is soil, sunlight, and water, but it must also withstand storms, droughts, and competition. Similarly, human growth depends on the capacity to engage with nature's challenges, learning from them and evolving through them. Nature presents hardships—hunger, storms, predators, illness—that are not barriers but invitations to become more. Hardship tests fitness and spurs innovation and adaptation. For early humans, the struggle to survive led to the invention of tools, fire, language, and communities. In facing the unpredictability of nature, humans developed resourcefulness, foresight, and cooperation.

Even today, those who immerse themselves in nature—mountaineers, explorers, farmers, conservationists—often report profound personal growth. They learn patience from the seasons, resilience from storms, and humility from the vastness of the wild. Growth, therefore, is not an escape from hardship but a transformation through it, and fitness is the bridge.

The body is the first instrument of growth. Nature demands physical engagement: walking, climbing, swimming, farming, etc. A fit body endures long efforts without collapse, heals quickly from wounds and sickness, and adapts to temperature changes and physical exertions. In ancient times, survival depended directly on physical fitness—the ability to hunt, gather, migrate, and build. Even in modern life, outdoor work, sports, and exercise build a body capable of growth. Physical engagement with nature strengthens the muscles and bones but also sharpens the senses, aligns biological rhythms with natural cycles, and fosters an intuitive understanding of natural processes. Thus, physical fitness becomes the soil where the seeds of growth are sown.

While the body grapples with the physical environment, the mind interprets, plans, and innovates. Mental fitness involves cognitive flexibility, problem-solving ability, creative imagination, patience, and focus. Nature constantly challenges the mind: finding paths through forests, predicting weather changes, constructing shelters. Early humans grew mentally fit by reading animal tracks, navigating by the stars, and observing seasonal changes. Even today, spending time in nature—hiking without maps, living off-grid—reawakens dormant cognitive skills like pattern recognition, memory, and improvisation.

Moreover, mental fitness cultivates humility. Nature does not yield to human will. Storms come despite forecasts. Animals behave unpredictably. Learning to adapt plans without panic or anger is mental fitness in action. Growth in nature sharpens the mind, making it less rigid, more aware, and more deeply connected to life's cycles.

Beyond the body and mind lies the heart—the center of emotions. Nature teaches patience and acceptance. Crops do not grow faster by worrying; rivers do not flow according to impatience. Emotionally fit individuals handle failure and disappointment with grace, remain calm in crises, and experience gratitude and wonder.

Nature is the greatest teacher of emotional resilience. A storm may ruin a field, a drought may wither a garden, but life persists. Observing such resilience cultivates inner strength. Time in nature reduces stress, anxiety, and depression, a fact now confirmed by modern science. Forest bathing, hiking, and time by the sea are proven to lower cortisol levels and enhance emotional well-being. The emotionally fit person learns from nature to flow with life's ups and downs rather than resist them—a lesson essential for genuine growth.

Beyond body, mind, and emotions lies the spirit—the dimension of meaning, purpose, and connection to something greater than oneself.

Nature, in its majesty and mystery, evokes spiritual reflection. The vastness of the ocean, the silence of a forest, the endless canopy of stars—these awaken a sense of wonder and transcendence.

Spiritually fit individuals find purpose beyond personal gain, experience awe, humility, and connectedness, and live with a sense of stewardship and gratitude. Many indigenous cultures have long recognized nature as sacred, seeing mountains, rivers, and trees not merely as resources but as living beings, teachers of wisdom. For a fit person, growth in nature involves deepening this spiritual awareness, seeing oneself not as a master of nature but as a participant in its grand unfolding.

Nature itself is filled with metaphors for growth. Trees grow slowly but firmly, weathering storms. Rivers find ways around obstacles. Seeds sprout in cracks in the pavement, teaching persistence. The fit person observes these patterns, internalizes them, and grows accordingly—developing resilience and patience like the tree, cultivating flexibility and persistence like the river, and finding opportunity even in adversity like the seed. Nature's growth is not hurried or forced; it is steady, organic, and graceful. Those who learn to grow likewise find enduring strength.

Growth is never a comfort zone; it lies on the edge of difficulty. In nature, animals adapt to new predators, plants adjust to changing climates, and ecosystems evolve after fires or floods. Similarly, humans grow most in response to challenges. Fitness is tested and strengthened in difficulty. Consider mountaineers who endure freezing winds and oxygen deprivation or farmers who persevere through floods and droughts. Their fitness—physical, mental, emotional—is honed through hardship, and their growth is proportional to the magnitude of their challenges. The fit person does not seek to avoid difficulty but to engage it creatively and courageously, trusting that growth lies beyond the struggle.

Yet modern civilization often shelters us from nature's trials. Climate-controlled rooms, processed food, and virtual experiences buffer us from direct engagement with the elements. While technology has eased certain hardships, it has also led to a disconnection from the natural processes that once shaped our growth. Without interaction with nature, physical fitness declines, mental sharpness diminishes, emotional resilience weakens, and spiritual connection fades. Reconnecting with nature—through outdoor activities, sustainable living, and mindful observation—restores these dimensions, revitalizing growth. Fitness, in this broader sense, is not a luxury; it is essential for authentic human flourishing.

True fitness and growth must align with ethical responsibility toward nature. Unrestrained exploitation leads not to growth but destruction—for both nature and humanity. The fit person understands that growth must be symbiotic, not parasitic, that stewardship of nature ensures long-term flourishing, and that true fitness includes responsibility and foresight. Sustainable practices—organic farming, renewable energy, conservation efforts—are modern expressions of fitness in action, ensuring that growth respects the delicate balance of ecosystems. In growing with nature, not against it, we ensure that both humanity and the natural world can thrive together.

Throughout history, those who harmonized fitness and nature achieved remarkable growth. Native American tribes lived in balance with forests, rivers, and plains, embodying physical endurance, environmental knowledge, and spiritual reverence. Mahatma Gandhi promoted simple living and self-sufficiency, reconnecting millions with natural rhythms. Modern conservationists like Jane Goodall demonstrate how deep engagement with nature leads to personal and global growth. These examples illustrate that fitness is not a solitary achievement but a communal, generational legacy of harmony with nature.

In an era of climate change, biodiversity loss, and ecological crisis, the call to grow fit with nature is louder than ever. Individuals can respond by spending time in wild places, learning traditional skills like gardening and herbal medicine, practicing mindfulness in nature, engaging in environmental activism, and living simply and sustainably. Such practices build the kind of fitness—physical, mental, emotional, spiritual, and ethical—that enables genuine growth.

The fit person does not conquer nature but grows within it—resilient as the oak, adaptable as the river, persistent as the seed. Fitness is not a static achievement but a dynamic dialogue with the world around us—a continuous dance of challenge and response, hardship and triumph, solitude and connection. To be fit is to be ready: ready to face the storm, climb the mountain, endure the drought, and rejoice in the rain. To grow in nature is not merely to survive but to thrive, to unfold one's fullest potential in step with the timeless rhythms of the earth.

As nature renews itself with each season, so too can the fit person renew body, mind, heart, and spirit—ever growing, ever becoming, ever rooted in the profound, enduring embrace of the natural world. Thus, we learn: the fit person can grow in nature—not despite it, but because of it.

❐

Chapter-10
In nature, life evolves by facing problems and overcoming challenges

Life, by its very nature, is unpredictable. No matter how carefully one plans or how diligently one prepares, problems and challenges will inevitably arise. This is not a flaw in the design of life but rather a fundamental characteristic of existence itself. Struggles are the crucible in which resilience is forged, and obstacles the proving grounds for personal growth. Yet, it is not merely the existence of problems that defines the trajectory of a person's life, but rather their approach to these challenges. Those who choose to face difficulties with ingenuity and sincere effort often discover pathways to success and fulfillment where others see only dead ends.

From ancient philosophical discourses to modern psychological studies, there is a unanimous agreement that problems are an inseparable part of human existence. Historical figures, regardless of their social or economic standing, encountered trials that tested their willpower and ingenuity. Change and uncertainty constantly accompany life; no one can control every external factor, and challenges invariably push individuals out of their comfort zones. Acknowledging this fundamental truth is the first step toward an empowered life. Denial or avoidance only exacerbates difficulties, while acceptance prepares the ground for proactive solutions.

When confronted with a challenge, the human mind typically reacts in one of three ways: fight, flight, or outsmart. Direct confrontation demands courage, avoidance ensures only temporary relief, but outsmarting requires strategic, thoughtful engagement with the problem. Outsmarting is not about trickery or shortcuts; it is about intelligent problem-solving—dissecting the problem into manageable parts, viewing it from multiple angles, and managing fear and anxiety with emotional intelligence. It often demands the maturity to step back and reassess rather than react impulsively.

While ingenuity provides the strategy, sincere efforts provide the fuel. Effort imbued with sincerity has persistence—the ability to continue despite setbacks; honesty—a clear and realistic appraisal of one's strengths and weaknesses; dedication—a commitment to the process, not just the outcome; and humility—the willingness to learn from failures and from others. Sincere efforts build character and create momentum, shifting the focus from external outcomes to internal growth, ensuring that even if the desired results are delayed, the individual is constantly progressing.

History and mythology both illuminate this principle. Thomas Edison, despite thousands of failed attempts before inventing the light bulb, exemplified the triumph of perseverance. Malala Yousafzai, surviving an assassination attempt, did not flee from her challenges but transformed them into a platform for advocacy, inspiring millions. Stephen Hawking, diagnosed with a debilitating disease at a young age, continued his research undeterred, contributing profoundly to the understanding of the cosmos.

Turning to Indian mythology, Arjuna on the battlefield of Kurukshetra faced a profound moral dilemma. Initially paralyzed by doubt and despair, he found clarity and strength through the wisdom imparted by Lord Krishna in the Bhagavad Gita, eventually fulfilling his duty with unwavering resolve. Lord Rama, unjustly exiled and burdened with immense trials, faced his adversities with patience, strategy, and adherence to dharma, culminating in his victory over Ravana. Dr. A.P.J. Abdul Kalam's journey from a humble beginning in Rameswaram to becoming the "Missile Man of India" and later the President is another testament to the power of perseverance, sincerity, and vision. These figures did not eliminate problems from their lives. They adapted, strategized, and made sincere efforts, demonstrating that the pathway to success often winds through adversity.

The logical process of confronting problems begins with acceptance—a refusal to waste time in denial. Analysis follows—breaking down the problem and identifying root causes rather than merely addressing symptoms. Strategic planning involves considering multiple solutions and weighing their merits. Once a plan is crafted, action must be taken with full dedication. Adaptation is crucial as new information emerges, and reflection ensures that lessons are learned for future challenges. This logical sequence is not a rigid formula but a dynamic process, evolving with each situation.

Resilience, the ability to recover from adversity, is not innate but cultivated. It requires optimism—the belief that challenges can be overcome; self-efficacy—confidence in one's problem-solving abilities; support systems—the guidance of friends, family, and mentors; and mindfulness—the awareness and regulation of one's emotional states. Bhishma Pitamah's unwavering patience and resolve, even as he lay grievously wounded on the bed of arrows awaiting the auspicious moment to depart from life, is a profound illustration of resilience. Through resilience, individuals maintain equanimity even when facing formidable obstacles.

However, there are common pitfalls that must be avoided. Procrastination magnifies problems; overconfidence underestimates challenges; negativity drains motivation and clouds judgment; and isolation—the rejection of help when available—reduces problem-solving capacity. Recognizing and avoiding these traps is crucial to maintaining steady progress.

At the heart of every successful confrontation with a problem lies a set of guiding values. Integrity demands acting honestly and ethically. Courage calls for facing fear with resolve. Patience teaches that worthwhile solutions take time. Lord Krishna's counsel to Arjuna in the Bhagavad Gita emphasized the importance of performing one's duty with courage and detachment—that steadfast values and unwavering effort are the true sources of victory. Values serve as the compass, orienting individuals in the right direction when the road becomes rough and confusing.

Cultural and historical perspectives from around the world echo this understanding. Stoicism from Greece teaches enduring hardship without complaint. Zen Buddhism from Japan emphasizes embracing impermanence and living in the present moment. The Bhagavad Gita advocates performing duty without attachment to results. In Indian history, Chanakya, the great strategist and teacher, exemplified pragmatic problem-solving. His sincere efforts and intellectual clarity led to the establishment of the Mauryan Empire, demonstrating how determination and strategic foresight can transform entire civilizations.

Each individual must customize their strategy according to their unique circumstances. Yet certain steps are broadly applicable. Self-assessment—understanding strengths, weaknesses, and resources; goal setting—defining what success looks like; resource mobilization—gathering information, tools, and support; strategic planning—developing a flexible plan; execution—acting with discipline and sincerity; and review and revision—adapting based on feedback and results. Personal growth and success are the byproducts of this iterative process.

In the final analysis, problems and challenges are not roadblocks but invitations to growth. They are not to be feared or avoided but to be engaged with intelligence and sincerity. Outsmarting challenges does not mean bypassing them but navigating through them with wisdom and effort. Those who accept this truth and dedicate themselves to sincere, intelligent action will not only find ways through their difficulties but will also find deeper purpose and resilience within themselves. Life, in its infinite complexity, will continue to present challenges, but with the right mindset and approach, the path forward will always be found.

As long as we live, the journey of confronting and overcoming challenges continues. Each victory builds confidence; each failure, if properly understood, builds wisdom. In this endless interplay of effort and outcome, the secret lies not in avoiding struggle but in mastering the art of facing it with sincerity and strategy. In doing so, we do not merely find a way; we find *our* way—a path uniquely shaped by our struggles, triumphs, and unwavering efforts.

❐

Chapter-11

You can make a hell of heaven—or a heaven of hell—through your perception

Problems in life possess a dual nature: objective and subjective. Objectively, every challenge has distinct elements—clear goals, tangible obstacles, required resources, and defined timeframes. A student preparing for the IAS examination faces an enormous syllabus; a businessman confronting market losses must wade through financial reports and strategies. These are external realities, factual and non-negotiable. However, objective difficulty alone does not govern how complex a problem feels. The very same IAS syllabus or financial downturn can appear overwhelming to one individual and manageable to another.

Subjective perception plays an even more profound role. Emotional stability, mental clarity, past experiences, belief systems, and resilience influence how challenges are experienced. In the Bhagavad Gita, Arjuna, standing before battle, perceived his duty as insurmountable. Emotionally crippled, he contemplated renunciation. Yet Krishna, offering a shift in perspective, taught him to perform his duty without attachment to outcomes. This change of vision transformed paralyzing despair into focused action. The battlefield did not change—Arjuna's mind did. Thus, problems are not just what they are; they are also how we see them.

Despite this understanding, people frequently entangle themselves in unnecessary complexities. Emotional overload is a primary cause. Fear amplifies risks, anxiety clouds reasoning, and anger provokes rash decisions. A person who loses their job might spiral into panic, envisioning a bleak, inescapable future, when a composed mind could calmly chart a new course. Emotional turbulence adds layers of difficulty to what could have been a straightforward challenge.

Beyond emotions, cognitive biases complicate life further. Catastrophizing convinces individuals that a single failure spells permanent defeat. Overgeneralization leads one to extrapolate a single setback into a sweeping judgment about life. Black-and-white thinking erases nuances, forcing choices between extreme alternatives. A student failing one exam may wrongly believe success is forever out of reach. Such distortions twist manageable hurdles into monstrous walls.

Modern psychology affirms that cognitive biases, unless managed, cloud judgment and exacerbate stress. Without prioritization, problems also swell uncontrollably. When everything appears equally urgent, energy scatters, and overwhelm follows. An entrepreneur attempting to boost sales, expand markets, develop products, and resolve HR issues simultaneously ends up exhausted and ineffective. As Confucius remarked, "He who chases two rabbits catches neither." Focus brings clarity; lack of it breeds confusion.

Overthinking is another trap. Endless cycles of "what if" create imaginary obstacles. Instead of acting, the mind spins in webs of hypothetical scenarios. In the Ramayana, Hanuman, tasked with crossing the ocean to Lanka, did not waste time analyzing; he remembered his latent power and leapt. His simplicity of action triumphed where hesitation would have failed.

Given these complexities, how does one simplify problems?

One method is to break challenges into smaller, manageable parts. The mind can handle defined tasks more effectively than it can handle vast, amorphous goals. Writing a book, for instance, becomes less daunting when broken down: outlining chapters, writing 500 words a day, editing one chapter each week. The strategy of divide and conquer underpins every successful project management system.

Prioritization is equally crucial. Not all problems carry equal weight. Identifying the vital few among the trivial many enables focused action. The Pareto Principle teaches that 80% of outcomes arise from 20% of causes. In the Mahabharata, Krishna directed the Pandavas to focus their strength on defeating pivotal warriors like Bhishma and Karna, a strategy that ultimately led to victory.

Emotional regulation is another cornerstone of simplification. A calm mind perceives reality more accurately. Ancient Indian practices—*dhyana* (meditation), *pranayama* (breath control), and self-inquiry—help regulate emotions and clear mental clutter. Scientific studies affirm that mindfulness meditation enhances emotional balance and cognitive clarity, leading to better problem-solving.

Seeking guidance can also strip away unnecessary complications. External advice offers fresh, detached perspectives. Modern CEOs rely on coaches and advisory boards for exactly this reason. In mythology, Arjuna's guidance from Krishna during his moment of crisis epitomizes how wise counsel can simplify internal turmoil.

Limiting options further eases decision-making. Behavioral economics speaks of the paradox of choice: an abundance of options often leads to paralysis and dissatisfaction. Reducing choices simplifies decisions and reduces stress. Steve Jobs famously wore the same style of clothing every day, conserving mental energy for more important tasks.

History, mythology, and modern examples all show the value of simplicity. Abraham Lincoln, during the American Civil War, faced a fractured nation, yet he focused unwaveringly on preserving the Union. His clarity simplified countless political dilemmas and culminated in the Emancipation Proclamation. Had he attempted to appease all factions, the war might have dragged on indefinitely.

Philosophy has long extolled the virtues of simplicity. Vedanta teaches that human suffering stems from identification with the transient, ever-changing world of Maya. By discerning the eternal Self (*Atman*) from this transient reality, unnecessary suffering dissolves. Problems belong to the body-mind complex, not to the true Self. Awareness of this distinction leads to less emotional upheaval and greater clarity. *Nididhyasana*—deep contemplation—clears the mental fog, unveiling the simplicity that lies at the heart of existence.

The Buddha's Middle Path advocates a life of balance, avoiding extremes of indulgence and asceticism. His Eightfold Path guides adherents toward right action and right mindfulness, fostering a present-centered awareness that dissolves complexity. When anchored in the now, past regrets and future anxieties lose their hold.

Stoicism mirrors these insights. Marcus Aurelius, the Roman emperor and Stoic philosopher, taught that we have power over our minds but not over external events. By focusing on internal virtues—courage, justice, temperance, wisdom—one can meet external chaos with serene simplicity.

In today's world, simplicity is more needed than ever. Information overload—news, social media, endless notifications—saturates the mind. Managing this influx through curated information, fixed times for consumption, and digital detoxes clears mental space, allowing for deeper thought.

Career choices have multiplied, leaving many young professionals paralyzed by indecision. Clarifying core values, identifying strengths, and aligning with long-term goals simplifies decision-making and fosters sustained success.

Even personal relationships, often entangled in poor communication and unmet expectations, benefit from simplicity. Open dialogue, active listening, clear boundaries, and the practice of forgiveness untangle complex relational knots. Simple communication, as stories in the Panchatantra show, often resolves conflicts that intricate schemes cannot.

Despite its virtues, simplicity faces challenges. The ego, desiring to feel important, prefers complex solutions over simple ones. True wisdom lies in choosing effectiveness over impressiveness and valuing clarity over complication.

Fear of missing out drives many to overcommit, complicating life unnecessarily. Simplifying demands the courage to say no and focus on fewer, more meaningful pursuits.

Finally, simplicity must not be confused with oversimplification. True simplicity requires deep understanding and careful selection of essentials without sacrificing critical details. As Einstein wisely observed, *"Everything should be made as simple as possible, but not simpler."*

Life's challenges are inevitable, but their complexity is a choice. Through conscious effort, overwhelming problems can be transformed into manageable tasks. Simplification is not a form of avoidance; it is a mark of mastery—the art of discerning what truly matters.

When Arjuna, during his archery training, focused solely on the eye of the bird, ignoring its feathers and surroundings, he achieved perfect aim. This encapsulates the essence of simplification: clarity of focus, calmness of mind, and courageous action.

Ultimately, the choice remains ours: to complicate life with fear, overthinking, and ego, or to simplify it with clarity, discipline, and wisdom. The external world may stay the same, but our internal world—the true battlefield—determines whether we live burdened or free. Thus, while facing challenges and solving problems, one can make them as complicated or as simple as one chooses—and in that choice lies the power to shape one's destiny.

❐

Chapter-12

Nothing hinders personality development more than ego and inertia—they are its most formidable enemies

Ahankara (ego) generates feeling of specific "I" and "mine", **kama** (selfish desire), **krodha** (anger), **mada** (pride), **moha** (attachment), **lobha** (greed), and **alasya** (inertia), which constitute **vikaras** (moral distortions) in an individual's life.

The Negative Impact of desire on the Personality of an Individual

Desire is a powerful and primal force that lies at the heart of human existence — it propels ambition, inspires action, and ignites the spark of creativity. Yet, not all desires are born equal. They fall into two distinct categories: selfish and unselfish. Selfish desire seeks personal gain at the cost of others, often breeding division, exploitation, and unrest. In contrast, unselfish desire aspires to rise together — it envisions progress that uplifts not just the self, but the whole. It is inclusive, expansive, and life-affirming. While unselfish desire builds, heals, and harmonizes, selfish desire isolates, corrodes, and ultimately disrupts the social fabric. One nurtures the soul of humanity; the other gnaws at its roots.

At its root, desire is a craving for something we believe will complete or fulfill us — wealth, status, power, love, or material possessions. The problem arises when the mind becomes obsessed with attaining these objects, seeing them as essential to happiness and self-worth. This obsession narrows the individual's perspective, making them blind to the broader realities of life. An individual dominated by selfish desire begins to judge every situation based on personal gain, losing objectivity and the ability to act with fairness and compassion.

One of the most damaging effects of selfish desire is emotional imbalance. When a person becomes overly attached to their selfish desire, they experience anxiety, restlessness, and dissatisfaction. The mind constantly oscillates between hope and fear — hope of achieving the desired object and fear of losing it. This emotional turbulence disrupts inner peace and weakens mental stability.

Selfish desire also weakens moral and ethical standards. In the quest to fulfill selfish desires, individuals may justify dishonest or unethical behavior. Small compromises, made in pursuit of personal goals, gradually erode integrity. Lies, manipulation, and exploitation can become habitual. Such behavior not only harms others but also diminishes the individual's own sense of self-respect. A person whose character is weakened by selfish desires may achieve temporary success, but it is often at the cost of long-term inner fulfillment and social trust.

Furthermore, selfish desire fosters dependency. When happiness is tied to the fulfillment of external cravings, individuals lose their inner freedom. They become slaves to circumstances, people, and possessions, constantly seeking validation and gratification. True strength of personality comes from autonomy — the ability to remain content and stable irrespective of external conditions. Selfish desire chains the individual, making them vulnerable to every fluctuation of fortune.

Ultimately, selfish desire leads to dissatisfaction. No matter how much is attained, the mind under the grip of selfish desire always craves more. This endless cycle of wanting and acquiring leaves a persistent sense of emptiness. The individual, despite outward achievements, remains internally unfulfilled, restless, and discontented. In conclusion, while desire is natural, its unchecked growth negatively impacts the personality of an individual. It clouds judgment, disturbs emotional balance, corrodes moral values, fosters dependency, and leads to chronic dissatisfaction. True personality development lies not in the suppression of all desires, but in mastering them — cultivating inner contentment, self-awareness, and a balanced mind. Only then can a person evolve into a personality marked by peace, strength, and authenticity.

The Negative Impact of Anger on the Personality of an Individual

Anger is a powerful emotion, arising naturally in response to perceived threats, injustices, or frustrations. While occasional anger can be constructive when it motivates corrective action, uncontrolled and habitual anger has a deeply corrosive effect on the personality of an individual. Over time, it distorts thinking, erodes emotional balance, harms relationships, and undermines personal growth. One of the first casualties of persistent anger is rational thinking.

Anger clouds judgment and narrows perception, making it difficult for individuals to view situations objectively. Under its influence, people tend to react impulsively, exaggerate minor provocations, and misinterpret others' intentions. This impaired judgment leads to poor decision-making, often resulting in regret and long-term consequences. A person whose mind is habitually agitated by anger struggles to maintain clarity, patience, and understanding — qualities essential for a mature and composed personality.

Emotionally, anger is highly destabilizing. Chronic anger keeps individuals in a constant state of tension and agitation. They are more likely to experience irritability, anxiety, and mood swings. Over time, this emotional turbulence can lead to deeper issues such as chronic stress, depression, or a sense of helplessness. Emotional instability, in turn, affects how one interacts with others, leading to frequent conflicts and misunderstandings.

Relationships suffer greatly under the influence of unchecked anger. Communication becomes harsh, empathy diminishes, and trust erodes. Friends, family members, and colleagues may begin to distance themselves, finding interactions with an angry person stressful and unpleasant. As social bonds weaken, feelings of loneliness and isolation may set in, further feeding frustration and resentment. A personality dominated by anger often loses the warmth, kindness, and patience necessary for healthy, enduring relationships.

Furthermore, anger fosters a negative self-image. After angry outbursts, individuals often feel guilt, shame, or regret, recognizing that they have hurt others or acted against their better judgment.

This cycle of outburst and regret can diminish self-esteem and self-confidence. Over time, the individual may begin to view themselves as incapable of self-control, which hampers efforts toward personal and professional growth.

From a broader perspective, anger also obstructs the development of virtues like compassion, forgiveness, and humility — traits that enrich character and inspire respect. A personality gripped by anger becomes rigid, judgmental, and intolerant, shutting the doors to learning, adaptation, and self-improvement.

In conclusion, while anger is a natural emotion, its unchecked presence has a profoundly negative impact on the personality of an individual. It impairs judgment, destabilizes emotions, damages relationships, erodes self-esteem, and blocks the path to inner growth and fulfillment.

To nurture a balanced and resilient personality, it is essential to recognize anger, understand its triggers, and cultivate practices such as mindfulness, empathy, and patience. Mastery over anger not only preserves personal well-being but also strengthens the foundations of a strong, peaceful, and admirable personality.

The Negative Impact of Pride on the Personality of an Individual

Pride is often viewed as a natural emotion, stemming from a sense of accomplishment or self-worth. While a moderate sense of pride can promote confidence and dignity, excessive pride — when it turns into arrogance or superiority — has a profoundly negative impact on the personality of an individual. It distorts perception, disrupts emotional balance, damages relationships, and impedes personal and spiritual growth.

At its core, excessive pride clouds self-perception. A proud individual tends to overestimate their abilities and worth, believing they are superior to others. This inflated self-image blinds them to their flaws and weaknesses, making self-improvement difficult. Constructive criticism is dismissed, and feedback is seen as an attack rather than an opportunity to learn. Over time, this distorted self-view leads to stagnation, as the individual resists change and refuses to acknowledge the need for growth.

Emotionally, pride fosters rigidity and hypersensitivity. A proud person craves admiration and validation but reacts defensively to any perceived slight. Small criticisms can evoke outsized reactions of anger or resentment. This emotional fragility disrupts inner peace and keeps the mind in a constant state of tension. Pride also blocks empathy, making it difficult for individuals to genuinely connect with others. They often view interactions through a lens of competition rather than cooperation, further isolating themselves.

Relationships, too, suffer under the weight of pride. Arrogant behavior alienates friends, family, and colleagues. A proud person may appear dismissive, condescending, or intolerant, creating an environment where others feel undervalued or disrespected. Over time, this erodes trust and goodwill, leading to isolation. Relationships thrive on humility, mutual respect, and the willingness to accept others' viewpoints — all qualities pride suppresses.

Moreover, excessive pride impedes personal and professional growth. It discourages curiosity and openness, qualities essential for learning and adaptation. A proud individual often believes they already possess all necessary knowledge or skills, closing themselves off from new experiences and perspectives. In professional settings, this attitude can lead to stagnation or even failure, as adaptability and continuous learning are critical for long-term success.

On a deeper level, pride obstructs spiritual and moral development. Many philosophical and religious traditions, from Stoicism to the teachings of the Bhagavad Gita, warn against the dangers of pride. True wisdom requires humility — the recognition that no matter how much one knows or achieves, there is always more to learn and higher ideals to strive for. Excessive pride strengthens the ego, fostering a false sense of self-sufficiency that distances individuals from deeper truths about themselves and the world.

In conclusion, while a balanced sense of pride can be healthy, unchecked pride has a corrosive effect on personality. It distorts self-perception, breeds emotional instability, damages relationships, and hinders both personal and spiritual growth. Cultivating humility, openness, and self-awareness is essential for overcoming the pitfalls of pride and developing a personality that is not only strong but also wise, compassionate, and respected by others.

The Negative Impact of Greed on the Personality of an Individual

Greed — the insatiable selfish desire for more wealth, power, or possessions — is a force that can silently corrode the core of an individual's personality. While ambition and aspiration are natural and even necessary for progress, greed goes beyond healthy ambition. It blinds individuals to ethical considerations, destabilizes emotions, damages relationships, and ultimately leads to inner dissatisfaction.

One of the most immediate impacts of greed is the distortion of values. In the grip of greed, individuals begin to prioritize acquisition over principles. Honesty, compassion, and fairness often become secondary to personal gain. To fulfill their endless cravings, people may resort to manipulation, deceit, or exploitation. Over time, this compromise erodes the moral foundation of the personality. The individual, once perhaps upright and fair-minded, becomes hardened and self-serving, gradually losing respect both for themselves and from others.

Emotionally, greed breeds restlessness and chronic dissatisfaction. No matter how much is acquired, the greedy mind always craves more. Successes bring only fleeting satisfaction before new selfish desire s arise. This endless cycle leads to frustration, anxiety, and even despair. Instead of enjoying achievements, the individual remains trapped in a state of perpetual want, unable to appreciate what they have. Inner peace and contentment — essential components of a balanced personality — are sacrificed at the altar of endless accumulation.

Greed also has a corrosive effect on relationships. It fosters a self-centered approach where others are seen not as individuals to connect with but as tools or obstacles in the pursuit of personal goals. Trust, mutual respect, and empathy — the foundations of healthy relationships — are undermined. Friends, family, and colleagues may begin to feel used or neglected, leading to isolation and broken bonds. The greedy individual, despite acquiring external wealth or success, often ends up emotionally impoverished and alone.

Furthermore, greed narrows the mind and stunts personal growth. A personality dominated by greed becomes fixated on material gain, leaving little room for intellectual, emotional, or spiritual development. The broader human qualities — generosity, creativity, empathy, wisdom — are neglected. Greed binds the individual to a superficial existence, preventing the deeper exploration of life's meaning and purpose.

Philosophical and spiritual traditions across cultures have long warned against the dangers of greed. Buddhism identifies it as one of the three poisons of the mind; Hindu scriptures speak of greed as a cause of bondage and suffering; Stoicism teaches that true happiness lies in desiring less, not more. These teachings emphasize that lasting fulfillment arises not from accumulation but from contentment, self-awareness, and ethical living.

In conclusion, greed, when left unchecked, has a profoundly negative impact on the personality of an individual. It distorts values, breeds emotional turmoil, damages relationships, and hinders true personal growth. Overcoming greed requires cultivating contentment, practicing generosity, and shifting focus from endless acquisition to meaningful living. Only then can a person develop a personality that is not only successful but also balanced, compassionate, and deeply fulfilled.

The Negative Impact of Attachment on the Personality of an Individual

Attachment — the emotional dependence on people, objects, or outcomes — is a natural part of human life. It arises from a sense of connection and the desire for security and continuity. However, when attachment becomes excessive or unhealthy, it exerts a profound negative impact on an individual's personality. It distorts perception, breeds emotional instability, hampers personal growth, and ultimately leads to suffering and dissatisfaction.

At its core, attachment binds individuals to the external world, making their happiness dependent on conditions beyond their control. A person who is deeply attached to relationships, possessions, or even personal achievements often lives in constant fear — fear of loss, change, or failure. This fear disturbs the inner peace and emotional balance essential for a healthy personality. Instead of being calm and resilient, the individual becomes anxious, insecure, and overly reactive to circumstances.

Attachment also clouds judgment. When deeply attached, people often view the object of their attachment through an idealized lens, ignoring flaws and exaggerating virtues. This distorted perception affects decision-making.

Individuals may make choices based not on reason and clarity but on emotional dependency. For example, attachment to a toxic relationship can prevent a person from recognizing harmful patterns and taking necessary action. Over time, such emotional blindness weakens the individual's ability to think critically and act decisively.

Furthermore, attachment fosters possessiveness and control. The individual tries to cling to people or things, resisting the natural flow of change. In relationships, this possessiveness can suffocate the other person, leading to tension and conflict. Instead of fostering love and respect, attachment breeds jealousy, insecurity, and fear of abandonment. These negative emotions erode the quality of personal interactions, turning what could be sources of joy into sources of pain.

Another significant impact of attachment is the stunting of personal growth. Growth requires openness to change, the courage to let go of the familiar, and the willingness to step into uncertainty. Attachment, by contrast, creates rigidity. Individuals bound by attachment cling to comfort zones, resist new experiences, and avoid risks. This resistance limits their potential, keeping them trapped in a narrow and often stagnant existence.

From a spiritual and philosophical standpoint, attachment is seen as a major obstacle to liberation and true happiness. Teachings from the Bhagavad Gita, Buddhism, and Stoicism emphasize the importance of detachment — not indifference, but a balanced engagement with the world without clinging. Detachment allows individuals to enjoy life fully without being enslaved by it, fostering inner freedom, clarity, and peace.

In conclusion, while some degree of attachment is natural, excessive attachment negatively impacts the personality of an individual. It disturbs emotional balance, clouds judgment, damages relationships, and hampers personal growth. Cultivating detachment — the ability to love and engage without clinging — leads to a stronger, freer, and more resilient personality. In detachment lies the secret of maintaining inner peace while navigating the inevitable changes of life.

The Negative Impact of Inertia on the Personality of an Individual

Inertia, in its simplest sense, is the resistance to change. While it is a natural principle in the physical world, when it governs human behavior, it becomes a serious obstacle to personal growth and development. Inertia in an individual manifests as an unwillingness to act, adapt, or improve. Over time, this resistance to movement erodes not only the opportunities that life offers but also the essential qualities that constitute a strong and dynamic personality.

A person trapped in inertia becomes passive, avoiding the efforts necessary for progress. They hesitate to step out of their comfort zone, clinging to familiar routines and habits even when they are counterproductive. This habitual inaction gradually breeds mediocrity. Life demands active participation, learning, and continuous adaptation, but inertia locks an individual in a state of mental and emotional stagnation. As a result, creativity diminishes, enthusiasm wanes, and the will to improve is paralyzed.

One of the most damaging effects of inertia is its impact on self-confidence. When a person consistently avoids taking action or facing challenges, they start to doubt their own capabilities. Small failures seem overwhelming, and even minor obstacles appear insurmountable. This loss of confidence can lead to a cycle of passivity and low self-esteem. An individual who once had potential and aspirations finds themselves stuck in a life of unfulfilled dreams and silent regrets.

Inertia not only affects personal ambitions but also damages relationships. Active engagement is the foundation of meaningful human connections. A person dominated by inertia often becomes indifferent or unreliable. They may withdraw from social responsibilities, fail to nurture friendships, or resist contributing to collective endeavors. Gradually, this leads to isolation, as others perceive them as disinterested or disengaged.

Moreover, inertia clouds the mind. It fosters laziness, procrastination, and a lack of mental alertness. Opportunities are ignored, and life becomes a passive experience rather than an active journey. The individual stops striving for excellence and settles for the bare minimum, depriving themselves of the joy of achievement and growth.

Breaking free from inertia requires conscious effort, discipline, and the willingness to embrace discomfort. It demands a commitment to action, however small the initial steps might be. Building momentum against inertia fosters resilience, adaptability, and a proactive attitude — qualities that are the backbone of a strong personality.

A dynamic personality is not defined by static comfort but by the ability to move, learn, and evolve. Overcoming inertia leads to renewed self-confidence, mental agility, and emotional strength. It opens the door to opportunities, deeper relationships, and a life of fulfillment.

In conclusion, inertia is not merely a lack of action; it is a silent force that erodes the essence of one's personality. If left unchecked, it can turn a promising life into one of quiet despair and wasted potential. Recognizing the grip of inertia and taking deliberate steps to overcome it is essential for anyone who aspires to live a meaningful and impactful life.

❒

Chapter-13

Detachment from the Unnecessary, Attachment to the Meaningful — A Guiding Law for Life

Life, in its purest essence, is not a matter of accumulation, but of alignment. Nature reveals this quietly, powerfully, and consistently. The roots of a tree do not stretch in all directions; they dig where nourishment is found. In the natural world, there is no confusion between what is essential and what is not. Everything that lives, grows, or flows follows an inner compass—guided not by chaos, but by necessity, by purpose, by life itself.

Human life, however, often loses this compass. In our pursuit of more—more opinions, more possessions, more validation—we forget to ask the only question that matters: is this truly necessary for my evolution? The cost of this forgetfulness is steep. It shows in our mental exhaustion, our emotional restlessness, our sense of dissatisfaction despite abundance. We are not starved of opportunities—we are overwhelmed by irrelevance.

We confuse noise with information, motion with progress, attention with meaning. In doing so, we drift from the rhythm of nature into the chaos of distraction. The real tragedy of modern life is not that people fail—it is that they succeed at things that do not matter. And this misplaced success, this triumph over the trivial, leads to an invisible failure of spirit.

What is needed, urgently and universally, is a return to what may be called the Law of Detachment from the Unnecessary and Attachment to the Meaningful—a law not made by humans, but etched into the very design of nature. This law is not a rule to be obeyed under pressure; it is a truth to be recognized through awareness. It is the difference between surviving like cluttered vines and growing like the banyan. It is the difference between living efficiently and living profoundly.

Detachment, in this context, does not mean indifference. It means intelligent discernment. It means recognizing that every moment of attention we spend on the unimportant is a moment we steal from the important. And what is important is not hidden or abstract—it is always present, always calling. The human body knows this. It does not waste blood on a broken limb. The mind, however, lacks such discipline—unless trained through reflection and restraint.

This confusion between what matters and what merely appears to matter is the core of all suffering. Stress is not born from action; it is born from wasted action. Anxiety does not come from lack of choice; it comes from choosing wrongly again and again. People are not tired because they work hard—they are tired because they work on things that drain but do not nourish. Like a river that has forgotten its direction, we spread wide but remain shallow.

If we could reorient ourselves, even slightly, the change would be profound. Imagine a life where energy is not scattered, where days are not cluttered with petty quarrels and shallow pursuits, where the heart is not burdened by comparison or jealousy, where the mind is not haunted by what others think, but focused on what truly must be done. Such a life is not a utopia. It is entirely possible—because it is how nature already lives.

Nature is the original master of prioritization. In winter, the tree sheds its leaves—not because it is dying, but because it is preserving life. In the dry season, animals migrate—not out of fear, but out of wisdom. In drought, the cactus does not bloom—but it survives. Every action in nature is based on the sacred logic of necessity and relevance. And so must be human action—if it hopes to align with peace, efficiency, and fulfillment.

Indian philosophy, especially Advaita Vedanta, takes this one step further. It does not merely ask what is useful—it asks what is ultimately real. The concept of *viveka*, the power of discrimination, is not simply about choosing between good and bad. It is about discerning between the eternal and the ephemeral. The wise do not chase what fades; they anchor themselves in what lasts. And this discernment is not mystical—it is intensely practical. Ask: Will this thought, this task, this argument matter five years from now? Will this conversation deepen my purpose? Will this habit make me freer or more entangled?

Without such questioning, we remain consumers of time. With it, we become creators of destiny.

Emotionally too, this law liberates us. A person who is attached to every comment, every judgment, every passing insult, is like a tree trying to catch every wind. Such a life is impossible. Nature shows us that stillness is not passivity—it is strength. The mountain does not respond to every storm. The sky does not resist the clouds—it lets them pass. This emotional poise comes not from suppression but from clarity: not everything deserves our attention, not every flame needs to be fanned.

The power of detachment lies in its quiet discipline. You do not need to announce that you are withdrawing. You simply stop feeding what drains you. Detachment is not visible; its fruit is visible—calm, clarity, and centered strength. It allows you to respond where needed, and remain unmoved where not.

But detachment alone is incomplete. Nature does not survive merely by rejecting the unnecessary. It thrives by embracing the essential. The river follows gravity. The seed cracks open for light. Similarly, we must not only withdraw from distraction—we must attach ourselves with full devotion to what gives meaning. Health, deep learning, compassionate work, noble relationships, spiritual practice, and silence—these are not luxuries. They are lifelines. They are not things to fit into life—they are life.

To attach oneself to these is to invest in one's highest possibility. To water these roots is to ensure that the fruit of peace and purpose will come in season. A person who reads, reflects, prays, helps, nurtures, and walks amidst trees is not withdrawing from the world—they are becoming its healer.

Such a life demands practice. It begins by refusing to start the day in haste. It deepens by checking: Is this activity worthy of my attention? Will this deepen or dilute me? It matures by letting go—physically and mentally—of what is excessive, overstimulating, or misaligned. And finally, it blossoms in the quiet conviction that we are not here to do everything—we are here to do the few right things, rightly.

Spiritually, this law is the root of liberation. The Gita teaches that detachment is not about leaving the world; it is about not being bound by it. Work, speak, love—but like the lotus in water: touched, but not tainted. Attach yourself to truth, to dharma, to that quiet inner witness that does not flicker with success or failure. Let the world change—be the stillness inside it.

This is not theory—it is practice. Every moment offers the choice. React or reflect. Accumulate or simplify. Please others or honor truth. Fear judgment or follow dharma. Every choice sculpts our soul.

In this sculpture, detachment is the chisel, and attachment to the essential is the vision. Let us not be shapeless stones carried by opinion and noise. Let us be statues—carved by clarity, standing firm in simplicity.

Let us not walk through life carrying everything we picked up on the way. Let us walk like the wind—light, purposeful, moving toward the meaningful.

And let us remember: in the final accounting, life will not ask how many things we carried—but how deeply we lived, how consciously we chose, how lightly we walked, and how lovingly we stayed rooted in what truly matters.

❐

Chapter-14
The Ethics of Gain: Selfish vs. Unselfish Actions in Society

In nature, nothing grows by harming another without consequences. The river does not hoard its waters—it flows, nourishing all along its banks. The beehive does not thrive through theft but through collective effort and mutual nourishment. The forest does not reward the tree that takes most; it sustains the one that gives back to the soil. In this quiet, unspeaking world of wind, water, root, and wing, there is a moral logic deeper than language, older than scripture—a law of balance, of mutual upliftment, of ethical growth. It is from this law that the human conscience, too, must take its cue.

Human action, in all its complexity, often arises from desire. There is a desire to rise, to shine, to succeed, to accumulate. This desire in itself is not unnatural—it mirrors the instinct of the seed pushing toward the sun. Yet just as nature distinguishes between the flowering plant and the invasive weed by their impact on the environment, so too must we distinguish between good gain and bad gain by its effect on others. The question is not whether we grow, but whether our growth darkens or brightens the lives around us. When a man becomes wealthy by cheating others, it is no more a noble gain than a parasite swelling on the lifeblood of its host. It is growth, yes, but not life-affirming growth. It is success in the same way a forest fire spreads—impressive in scale, but barren in spirit.

True gain—what may be called good gain—is that which does not rob the world of its balance. It is the sunlight that touches many leaves, the wellspring that serves every root. It is when a person's prosperity uplifts others too; when one's success does not demand another's sorrow. The ethical worth of a gain lies not in its magnitude, but in its method. A small act done with integrity may be morally greater than a vast empire built on injustice.

In human civilization, the psychology of selfish gain often originates from a fragmented view of life—a belief that the world is a battlefield where only one can win. This zero-sum perspective breeds a sharp sense of separation: me versus them, my profit versus their loss, my victory through their defeat. Such a worldview stands in contrast to nature's example, where coexistence is not weakness but wisdom. The tree does not grow by pushing others down—it finds its light. The stream does not dry up another to fill itself—it follows the path of least resistance, nourishing as it moves. When humans operate against this natural ethos—exploiting others, manipulating systems, consuming beyond need—they do not merely commit moral errors; they violate the deeper code of life.

History offers abundant proof. The colonial empires that grew rich by draining the lifeblood of other lands did not merely exploit economies; they fractured the harmony of entire civilizations. They gained, yes—but like a locust swarm gains: with devastation in its wake. That is not real gain—it is moral deficit dressed in the costume of progress. Likewise, in personal lives, when someone climbs the social ladder by deception, betrayal, or calculated cruelty, the soul pays a price far heavier than any medal can mask. Just as a diseased tree might look tall until the next strong wind uproots it, so too does selfish gain crumble in time.

In contrast, unselfish gain grows like a healthy forest—quietly, cooperatively, and lastingly. It emerges from a worldview rooted in empathy and guided by wisdom. It is the recognition that one's well-being is not separate from the well-being of others. The one who lives by this law does not hoard the fruit of their labor, but shares its seeds. They understand that gain need not be solitary to be satisfying. It need not be exclusive to be excellent. It is possible—indeed natural—to rise by lifting, to lead by listening, to grow by giving.

When a group of farmers pools their harvest and profits together, when a teacher sees success not in salary but in the awakening of young minds, when a healthcare innovator lowers costs so the poor can live—these are not exceptions; these are echoes of how nature itself functions. The coral reef, the mycelial network beneath forests, the mutual aid of bird flocks and animal herds—these are not random alliances. They are sophisticated models of unselfish gain, where survival and success are bound not in domination, but in support.

Even in the corporate world, those who build inclusive enterprises, those who treat workers with fairness, those who design systems that serve society as well as shareholders—such people align more with the flow of nature than the tycoon who drains lands and labor only to hoard in vaults. The tree that bears sweet fruit is remembered, the one that overshadows all is often resented. The more we study nature, the more we see that the greatest strength lies not in the ability to take, but in the capacity to nourish.

Thus, if the question is: can we grow and remain ethical? Can we succeed and remain just? Can we gain and not destroy? The answer is found in every living thing around us. The ecosystem thrives because it is inclusive. The wind moves freely because it seeks no possession. The bird flies high because it travels light. There is no need to renounce ambition—but there is every need to redefine it. Let ambition be not about more, but about meaning. Let success not be counted in currency, but in contribution.

When our gain becomes the garden in which others may grow, when our rise becomes the staircase on which others climb, when our work becomes the water that quenches many roots—then we are no longer just individuals chasing personal dreams. We become part of the rhythm of nature itself. We become what we were meant to be—not masters of life, but participants in its sacred dance.

In a world that celebrates speed, let us admire direction. In a world that honors accumulation, let us seek harmony. In a world that tempts us to win at any cost, let us choose to win only if it blesses others too.

That is not weakness—it is wisdom. That is not loss—it is legacy. That is not less—it is life, as nature intended.

The forest does not grow because a single tree takes all the sunlight; it grows because each tree finds its light without stealing another's. The bee does not survive by hoarding all nectar, but by serving the flower and, in turn, the hive. Rivers do not choose only one bank to bless; they flow freely and fairly, nourishing both sides. Nature thrives not by selfishness, but by a quiet and unwavering principle of balance, reciprocity, and shared flourishing. This is not just a pattern in ecology—it is a moral law embedded in the very architecture of existence. It is the same law that Indian philosophy, economics, and political wisdom echo when they proclaim that unselfish gain is the only true gain, and that to rise at the cost of others is neither noble nor sustainable, but a disguised form of decay.

Indian philosophy, at its deepest, reflects this cosmic law of mutual upliftment. The *Bhagavad Gita* does not merely teach action—it prescribes selfless action, *Nishkama Karma*, as the purest form of engagement. Lord Krishna's exhortation to Arjuna is not to abandon the battlefield, but to engage in it without selfish attachment—not for personal glory, but for *Lokasangraha*, the welfare of the world. Just as the sun rises not for one village but for all, a *dharmic* (religious) individual acts not for personal gain alone but to uphold the balance of life. The Gita's verse— *"Tasmād asaktaḥ satataṁ kāryaṁ karma samācara..."* —is not just a spiritual command; it is a mirror of the law that governs the trees, the winds, and the tides. It teaches us to act without clinging, to serve without pride, and to earn without injury to others.

The *Upanishads* too remind us that life is meant to be lived in the spirit of *Yajna*—a sacred sacrifice where one partakes without possessiveness, where giving is not loss but the true form of receiving. In this light, *dharma* (religion) becomes not just a personal virtue but a collective obligation. A life lived against the good of others is a life lived against the order of the cosmos. One who hoards while others hunger, one who thrives while others are trampled, breaks not only social ethics but spiritual law. Growth that ignores this principle may seem powerful for a while, but like a tree grown in poisoned soil, it cannot stand the test of time.

The economy, too, mirrors these truths. When capitalism degenerates into ruthless accumulation—when profits are wrung from the labor of the underpaid, when industries poison rivers and skies, when companies evade social responsibilities—it may appear as economic strength, but it is ecological and ethical collapse in disguise. Monopolies, environmental destruction, exploitation of labor, and short-term greed create not wealth, but wounds. They are unnatural—unlike the forest, where no single species dominates, but all thrive through diversity and exchange. A business that grows by suppressing others acts like an invasive species—it may grow fast, but eventually disrupts the very ecosystem that sustains it.

Ethical capitalism, or what many now call conscious capitalism, is a return to nature's wisdom. A fair wage is not charity—it is sunlight shared equally. Environmental responsibility is not an obligation—it is the only way the forest continues to bloom. Community engagement is not brand-building—it is root-deep growth. A company that serves its workers, respects its consumers, sustains its environment, and reinvests in its community does not only do good—it ensures its own survival. The wise businessman is like the pollinator—his success lies in the fertility of others. His richness is measured not in hoarded currency but in the abundance he helps create around him.

The same principle extends into the social and political realm. A society where a few live in gold-plated isolation while many lack clean water or basic education cannot survive. The imbalance is not only unjust—it is unstable. Just as nature collapses when one species overtakes the rest, human societies implode when equity is lost. Democracies, public welfare systems, progressive taxation—all emerge from the understanding that development must not be like a vertical tower but like a growing tree, whose shade, fruits, and shelter reach all. The state, like the soil, must support the weakest roots if the whole forest is to remain standing. If the powerful use their gain only to build taller fences instead of wider bridges, unrest becomes inevitable. Revolutions do not begin in ideologies—they begin in hunger and humiliation.

But perhaps the most profound truth lies within the individual spirit. The unselfish person sleeps better. The one who gives, who uplifts, who includes, walks lighter—not because they have less, but because they carry no guilt, no fear, no secret shame. In contrast, the selfish gainer, even if rich, remains imprisoned—haunted by loss, chased by doubt, surrounded by suspicion, and isolated by mistrust. Spiritual psychology tells us what nature shows us every day: joy multiplies when shared, and peace grows where ego recedes. The happiest people are not those who have everything—but those who make others feel they have something too.

The law of karma, too, reflects nature's unfailing justice. Just as the seed sown determines the tree that grows, the actions taken today determine the fruits of tomorrow. One may gain through deceit or destruction, but such gain is hollow—it invites reversal. The exploitative businessman, the dishonest politician, the ruthless tycoon—all may rise, but their fall is already sown. Their *karma* is not delayed—it is merely ripening. Peace of mind, love from others, inner contentment—these are not gifts; they are rewards for ethical living. They cannot be stolen. They cannot be bought. Only the one who walks in tune with the larger order of life enjoys them. The karmic cycle is not punishment—it is correction. Nature restores what selfishness disrupts.

Ultimately, what emerges is not a moral suggestion, but a living truth: that shared prosperity is not just a noble dream—it is the only way to live sustainably, happily, and harmoniously. The moral of the forest is not competition but collaboration. The secret of the hive is not hoarding but harmony. The logic of the river is not ambition but flow. In a world torn by greed, division, and the illusion of isolated gain, we must return to this original wisdom: to gain at the cost of others is not gain, but theft; to grow while others wither is not success, but failure in disguise.

Let us then choose the path that nature walks every day. Let our gain be not a burden on others, but a blessing for all. Let our success be the sunrise that lights many paths, not the shadow that darkens others. Let us rise—not above—but with others.

For in the final unfolding of all things, the good life will not be measured by what we had, but by how many we helped flourish. The richest legacy is not gold—it is the green that grew in our wake.

❒

Chapter-15
The Mind—A Faithful Servant, But a Ruthless Master

In the ceaseless whirlwind of modern life, where haste has become habitual and silence a rarity, mental anxiety and illness have grown into silent epidemics. From the tremors of daily stress and anxiety to the tremors of depression and deeper psychological afflictions, the human mind finds itself increasingly besieged. Bombarded by external stimuli and entangled in internal conflicts, we drift between distraction and despair. Yet, amid this tempest, ancient spiritual traditions—Vedanta, Buddhism, and other Eastern philosophies—offer timeless insights into the nature of the mind and the essence of self. Their wisdom points not outward but inward, toward that still centre of awareness that lies untouched by the mind's turbulence.

At the heart of these teachings is the distinction between the *mind* and *pure consciousness*. Consciousness is not a product of thought, nor is it bound by sensation or memory. It is the silent witness—the immutable awareness that beholds all movements of body and mind without being moved itself. While the mind fluctuates like the restless sea, consciousness remains the calm depths beneath, ever-present and unchanging.

The mind, by contrast, is a wondrous yet fickle instrument. It is the seat of thoughts, emotions, memories, desire, and dreams. Endlessly active, it processes sensory input, interprets experience, and forms judgments. But it is also vulnerable—shaped by past conditioning, swayed by selfish desires, and disturbed by fears. In times of anxiety or mental illness, it is the mind that trembles and falters, clouding perception and entangling the self in suffering. When allowed to rule unchecked, the mind becomes a harsh master, enslaving us to its whims and fears. But when guided by higher awareness—when consciousness holds the reins—the mind becomes a faithful servant, capable of clarity, creativity, and peace.

Mental illness arises from many roots: genetic inheritance, trauma, environmental stressors, and unhealthy lifestyles. Anxiety, for instance, is often a response to imagined threats or unresolved tensions. It manifests as restlessness, fear, and obsessive worry, and when prolonged, it can lead to deeper disorders—panic attacks, chronic fatigue, or even physical ailments like hypertension. More complex conditions, such as depression, bipolar disorder, or schizophrenia, involve intricate imbalances of thought, emotion, and perception. Yet in all such afflictions, a common thread emerges—the unruly activity of the mind, which either magnifies suffering or, when calmed, paves the way to healing.

When the mind begins spinning stories of catastrophe, pause and bring in the light of reason. Ask yourself, "What is the most likely outcome?" More often than not, reality is gentler than our anxious imagination. Fear tends to exaggerate, but reason restores balance. Reframing the inner dialogue can be a powerful tool—don't surrender to despair with thoughts like, "Everything will go wrong." Instead, meet fear with faith: "Even if something does go wrong, I will rise to it with strength and grace." Let your mind find a path through fear, not around it.

Anxiety, though painful, can be an invitation to evolve. Don't see it as an enemy; see it as a furnace in which courage and wisdom are forged. Let go of the illusion of perfection. Progress is the true measure of growth. Celebrate even the smallest steps forward; each one is a tribute to your resilience.

Anxious thoughts often disguise themselves as absolute truths. But they are not facts—they are just thoughts. Recognize them for what they are. Label them gently: "This is just a thought." Let them drift by, like clouds in the sky—observed, but not clung to. Mindfulness trains us to witness without being consumed, to observe without judgment.

Much of anxiety stems from the desperate need to control what cannot be controlled. But peace is born not from grasping, but from letting go. Surrender to the unknown. You do not need certainty to be calm. What you can control—your breath, your presence, your response—these are enough. Embrace the truth that all emotions, even the most unsettling, are temporary visitors. Let them come. Let them go.

Anxiety thrives in imagined futures and replayed pasts. Its antidote is presence. Anchor yourself in the now—through deep breathing, grounding your senses in the world around you, and gently returning your attention to what *is*. Meditation, practiced even for a few minutes daily, can transform your relationship with the moment. For it is in the now that peace quietly waits.

Often, the anxious mind turns harshly against itself. Replace self-criticism with self-compassion. Speak to yourself as you would to a dear friend: "It's okay to feel this way. I'm doing the best I can." Recall your own strength—remember the storms you've already weathered. Let those memories be a reminder of your inner fortitude.

The endless cycle of "What if" questions rarely brings clarity. Instead, it deepens confusion and doubt. When your thoughts begin to spiral, pause and ask, "Is this thought helpful?" If not, gently let it go. If you must imagine the future, choose to envision healing rather than doom. The future is still unwritten. Let hope be part of the ink.

Learn to sit with uncertainty. Life itself is a mystery, and no amount of worry can change that. What you *can* change is your ability to adapt. Gently expose yourself to uncertainty—bit by bit. Over time, you will find strength where there once was fear. Resilience does not come from controlling outcomes but from trusting your capacity to meet them.

Anxiety often paralyzes, but action liberates. Even the smallest step toward a solution can shift your state of mind. Break large problems into manageable parts. Take the first step, however small. Worry circles endlessly; action moves forward. Ask yourself: "What can I do, right now, to move ahead?"

An anxious mind narrows its field of vision. Gratitude widens it. Start a simple habit—each day, write down a few things you're thankful for: a conversation, a moment of sunlight, a breath of fresh air. Gratitude softens the tension within. Even amid challenge, find something to honor. "I may be anxious, but I'm grateful for this chance to grow."

The anxious mind often deals in extremes: all or nothing, success or failure, good or bad. But life lives in the middle ground. Embrace the nuance of real experience. Replace absolutes like "I always fail" with truths like "Sometimes I struggle, but I also succeed." Speak to yourself not with tyranny, but with truth.

Understanding your anxiety begins with observing it. Watch for patterns—notice when and where it appears. Is it tied to certain situations, people, or pressures? Awareness is the first step toward mastery. And once you're aware of your triggers, you can prepare for them. Enter those spaces with calming tools—deep breaths, inner affirmations, or silent prayers.

Perfectionism is one of anxiety's oldest allies. But peace is found not in perfection, but in "good enough." Accept that your worth is not measured by flawless performance. What matters is your sincerity, your presence, your heart. Celebrate effort. Let your journey be guided by care, not comparison.

Anxiety whispers of doom; optimism replies with quiet faith. You don't need to believe everything will be perfect—only that something good is still possible. Recall the times you thought you couldn't go on, and yet you did. Let those memories remind you: You are stronger than fear, and more resilient than doubt.

Your mind becomes what you feed it. Choose nourishment over noise. In anxious moments, limit your exposure to fear-driven or sensational media. Protect your mental space like sacred ground. Fill it instead with beauty, calm, and kindness. Curate your environment to support your peace.

In the end, confronting anxiety is not about silencing fear forever. It's about walking through it—with awareness, compassion, and courage. It's about knowing that even in your most anxious moments, you are not broken—you are becoming. Every step you take in understanding your mind is a step toward freedom.

The mind is malleable, not fixed. With awareness, compassion, and consistent practice, it can be transformed from a restless adversary into a wise companion. Anxiety, though real and sometimes fierce, is not the end of the story—it is an invitation to greater presence, deeper resilience, and a more loving relationship with oneself.

Let your thoughts be kind. Let your focus be present. Let your soul be steady. The journey toward calm begins with a single breath.

In the swiftly shifting currents of the modern world, mental anxiety and illness have emerged as profound challenges—silent afflictions that touch lives across all boundaries. Yet amidst this growing storm, the interplay between *consciousness* and the *mind* offers a beacon of hope. At the heart of this healing lies a timeless truth: consciousness, as pure awareness, is the unmoving ground beneath the waves of thought, emotion, and experience. It is the silent witness, untouched by the mind's turbulence, from which clarity and peace may arise.

By cultivating *self-awareness*, grounding oneself in the *present moment*, and fostering *positive mental habits*, individuals begin the gentle but transformative process of easing anxiety. These practices do not merely mask symptoms; they reorient the inner life—awakening a deeper presence that watches, understands, and ultimately transcends the fluctuations of the mind.

The integration of consciousness with the practical functions of the mind offers a powerful and enduring path to mental well-being. It is a convergence of ancient spiritual wisdom and modern psychological insight, each echoing the other in its call to inwardness, clarity, and healing. Through this integration, the restless mind finds its master—not in force, but in awareness—and the soul discovers its sanctuary.

Overcoming anxiety is not a battle to be fought, but a journey to be walked—patiently, mindfully, with courage and compassion. It often begins by rewiring thought itself, gently challenging the assumptions we carry about the world, our struggles, and our own identity. By learning to embrace uncertainty, to speak to ourselves with kindness rather than judgment, and to question the catastrophic narratives that anxiety weaves, we begin to loosen its hold.

When these shifts in perspective are coupled with mindfulness, meditation, and practices that restore calm to body and spirit, a quiet resilience takes root. This resilience is not the absence of difficulty, but the presence of strength—the strength to meet life not with fear, but with grace.

In this light, the path to peace is not a distant promise, but a present possibility.

Life flows through us as energy—creative, destructive, or transformative. This energy takes shape through the mind, which, if left idle, turns dangerous. As the adage says, *"An empty mind is the devil's workshop"*—a timeless truth. A mind without purpose invites delusion, addiction, negativity, and despair.

The human mind is naturally very active. Left unchecked, it spirals into fear, fantasy, or self-destruction. Like stagnant water breeds disease, a stagnant mind breeds decay—fueling envy, anxiety, inertia, or even crime. Idleness doesn't relax the mind—it rots it.

Ancient scriptures and modern science agree. Krishna advised Arjuna to act without attachment. Buddha taught Right Effort. Marcus Aurelius emphasized purposeful living. Freud and Jung warned how idle energy turns toxic.

Today, digital distractions mask idleness as leisure. Endlessly scrolling, we numb the mind and lose clarity, agency, and joy. Excess screen time fuels anxiety and isolation, creating a silent crisis of disengagement.

The only cure is **constructive engagement**—meaningful work that directs the mind positively. This need not be career success alone. Reading, creating, helping, meditating, learning, and reflecting—all are nourishment for the mind. Purpose anchors energy and channels it toward growth.

A mind engaged in sincere effort is sharper, calmer, and healthier. It contributes to society, resists despair, and flourishes in creativity and peace. Education and parenting must emphasize purposeful habits, not idle entertainment. Spiritual practice and philosophical contemplation also offer depth and inner anchoring.

Engagement must become a daily discipline. Begin with small intentions, structure routines, and surround yourself with inspiration. The idle mind resists at first, but gradually transforms when aligned with purpose.

Neglecting this principle has social consequences too. Idle minds, especially among youth, can become breeding grounds for unrest, extremism, or nihilism. Societal peace depends on individual purpose.

In essence, the mind is a powerful force—if not fed with purpose, it will devour peace. Choose to engage it meaningfully. Let your mind be a temple of creativity, not a workshop of chaos. In that choice lies your strength, clarity, and peace. **Feed the mind with purpose—or it will feed on you.**

❐

Chapter-16

To survive and grow is a natural instinct—and the right to self-defense stands valid as long as the threat to life or reputation is real

To live is not merely a fact — it is a right. And this right, the very essence of existence, carries within it the inborn authority to protect itself. The instinct to survive is not taught. It is not learned from books, sermons, or laws. It is embedded in the very breath of life. The tree bends to avoid the storm. The bird flies away when danger nears. The child cries in fear before it can even speak. Every living being — from the crawling insect to the conscious human — carries an undeniable, sacred drive: to preserve itself and to evolve.

This instinct is not a sign of weakness. It is the source of strength. From the seed pushing through soil to reach sunlight, to the old man defending his honor against falsehood, every effort to protect and grow is a testimony to the vitality of life. It is a natural law, more ancient than any constitution, more primal than any philosophy: what exists has a right to continue, to flourish, and to guard its dignity.

Human beings, unlike other creatures, are gifted not only with physical faculties but also with mind, morality, and meaning. Therefore, the defense of life in humans is multidimensional. It is not limited to defending the skin and bones. It stretches far beyond — into the realm of dignity, truth, self-respect, reputation, and moral autonomy. When someone threatens not just your breath, but your name, your voice, your peace, and your honor — the need to defend is not just valid, it becomes sacred.

No society, however advanced, no law, however detailed, can be present in the exact moment when danger strikes. Therefore, the right of self-defense is not something society gives — it is something society must recognize. It belongs to the individual by the virtue of being alive. It is not borrowed from authority. It flows directly from the soul. And when there is a real threat — not imaginary, not exaggerated, but actual and immediate — to life or to reputation, the right to act, to speak, to protect, and even to resist with strength is not only permissible — it is necessary.

When a person is assaulted, when a woman is cornered, when a child is threatened, or when a citizen is defamed with lies, it is not violence to defend. It is courage. It is dharma. And this dharma is valid, legitimate, and righteous — so long as the threat exists. The moment danger fades, the sword must be sheathed. But while danger breathes, defense is not a sin — it is a duty.

Human history is replete with examples of individuals and civilizations who fell because they failed to defend. It is also illuminated by those who stood, sometimes alone, sometimes trembling, but stood firm when their life or honor was under siege. Their defense became their dignity. Bhagat Singh did not act for personal revenge — he responded to a nation's insult, to injustice that choked the breath of millions. His was not rebellion — it was defense of the spirit of a people.

In the present day, we witness journalists attacked for speaking the truth, whistleblowers losing jobs for defending public integrity, women resisting systemic harassment, and honest officers targeted for upholding law. These are not isolated cases of civil disobedience or disorderly conduct. These are modern-day manifestations of a timeless principle — that when truth is under siege, silence is betrayal. A journalist exposing corruption is defending the soul of democracy. A whistleblower revealing systemic rot is safeguarding public trust. A woman resisting harassment is asserting her fundamental right to dignity and safety. An officer who refuses to bow to political pressure is defending the very fabric of lawful governance. Their actions are not disruptions — they are ethical shields raised against the arrows of injustice. To mislabel such individuals as troublemakers is to turn morality on its head. It is to stand with the oppressor rather than with the defender of truth. These individuals are not the violators of order — they are the real protectors of balance, courage, and integrity in society.

And what about reputation? What about honor? Can it be ignored just because it is invisible? A person's name is their moral currency. Reputation, once attacked, can destroy lives more deeply than physical injury. When false allegations are spread, when social media is used as a weapon, when mobs vilify with no proof, the impact is as destructive as any weapon. In such cases, to remain silent is not peace — it is surrender. To respond — with truth, with dignity, with evidence, with courage — is the highest form of self-respect.

Law, too, understands this. In India, the Penal Code acknowledges your right to defend not just your life, but also your body, your property, your name — and even someone else's safety — when real danger is present. But it also reminds us: this right is not a weapon of revenge. It is a shield. The moment the threat ends, so must the act of defense. That boundary is what makes us civilized.

Defense becomes violence only when it continues beyond necessity. Defense becomes cruelty when it turns into punishment. Defense becomes unjust when it crosses the limits of reason. But within the moment of danger, the right to act, to speak, to push back, is as sacred as breath itself.

This principle is not confined to individual action. Nations too invoke it. A country invaded has the right to strike back — not out of hate, but to protect sovereignty. Families have the right to resist dishonor. Workers have the right to defend against exploitation. Whistleblowers have the right to speak truth to power. None of this is selfish. It is the purest form of self-respect — of survival and growth.

When someone tries to crush your potential, suppress your voice, or attack your integrity, know this — you are not required to accept it silently. Your resistance is not violence. It is a voice for life. You are not an aggressor when you defend. You are alive. Fully, righteously, and powerfully alive.

But this power must be exercised with clarity. Defend not out of fear, but from inner strength. Respond not with vengeance, but with determination. Use not lies, but truth. And when the storm passes, return to peace. The right of defense is like fire — it gives warmth when needed, but must not burn the house. Its greatness lies in its precision, its restraint, and its purpose.

Let us raise a generation that knows this truth — that living with dignity means standing firm when life, liberty, or reputation is under threat. That silence in the face of cruelty is not virtue. That nonviolence does not mean helplessness. That peace is not passivity. That one must grow, one must evolve — and that to do so, one must also protect what is rightfully theirs.

To survive is not cowardice. To defend is not aggression. To protect your inner and outer life is not sin. It is nature. It is conscience. It is dharma.

And remember always: this right of defense remains yours — until the danger remains real. Once the threat ends, peace must return. But while the threat breathes, you are not wrong to rise. You are right to resist.

For life is not meant to be lived in fear. It is meant to be lived in freedom, in truth, and in dignity. And if that freedom is ever endangered — rise. Speak. Act. Defend. And stand tall, knowing that nature itself stands with you.

In the final reckoning, the instinct to defend life is the instinct to honor life itself. Just as the flame protects its source from wind, just as the tree stretches against gravity to seek light, so too must the human soul push back against harm to preserve its truth. The right to self-defense is the echo of nature's deepest wisdom: that which is real protects itself. And when you act to defend, you are not opposing the world — you are aligning with the cosmos. To live with awareness, to respond with integrity, to protect with courage, and to restore peace with humility — this is the way of the wise, the just, and the free.

❒

Chapter-17

Lasting Happiness Comes from Sincere thinking and Working Only

Happiness — the elusive treasure that humankind has sought since time immemorial — remains the central aspiration of every individual. Philosophers have pondered it, religions have prescribed paths to it, and modern sciences have tried to measure and decode it. Yet, despite all the advancements, the essential truth remains unchanged: lasting happiness cannot be bought, inherited, or manufactured. It arises from within, born out of sincere work — the genuine engagement of mind, body, and spirit in meaningful action. It is not the fleeting thrill of achievement nor the momentary pleasure of indulgence but a deep, enduring contentment that only sincere effort can cultivate.

From ancient sages to contemporary thinkers, the link between sincere work and lasting happiness has been a constant refrain. Work, in its truest sense, is not merely a mechanical act of labor but an offering, a manifestation of purpose, discipline, and authenticity. When pursued sincerely, it becomes a spiritual exercise that elevates the doer beyond the mundane struggles of existence, into a realm where happiness is not something pursued but something realized.

In the natural world, every being engages in some form of sincere work. The bird building its nest, the ant carrying food back to its colony, the tree silently laboring to grow — each fulfills its nature through persistent, undistracted effort. There is no pretense, no procrastination, no self-deception. In fulfilling their inherent tasks, they maintain the harmony of the ecosystem and, in doing so, partake in the quiet joy of existence. Human beings, with their complex consciousness, have the capacity to engage in work not merely for survival but for meaning. It is in this sincere engagement that true and lasting happiness is found.

Sincere work is characterized by wholeheartedness. It demands the full presence of the worker — the mind focused, the heart involved, the body committed. In a world increasingly driven by appearances and shortcuts, the value of such engagement is often underestimated. Superficial effort may yield temporary rewards, but it fails to nourish the soul. Only when one's labor is honest and wholehearted does it sow the seeds of true happiness.

Consider the craftsperson who shapes wood into beautiful furniture, not to rush through the process, but to honor the material and the craft itself. Every stroke of the chisel, every smoothing of the surface, carries a piece of the artisan's soul. There is a rhythm to such work, a harmony between hand and mind, that transcends the task itself. The result, whether recognized or not, is secondary; the process itself becomes a source of deep satisfaction. In such sincere work lies the secret of lasting happiness.

Contrast this with labor done under compulsion, without interest or honesty. Work that is motivated by external rewards alone — money, fame, or power — may lead to moments of excitement or brief periods of success, but it cannot sustain happiness. The heart grows restless, the mind dissatisfied, and the soul weary when work is divorced from sincerity. Such labor, no matter how lucrative, leaves a hollow feeling — a sense that something vital has been lost.

Sincerity in work aligns action with inner values. When one's labor reflects personal principles and true intentions, it brings an integrity that shields against the chaos of the world. The individual who works sincerely sleeps well, unburdened by guilt or regret. There is no need for pretension, no fear of exposure, no gnawing anxiety about being judged. In sincerity lies a freedom that external success can never match. It allows a person to live authentically, and authenticity is the wellspring of lasting happiness.

The importance of sincere work is a central tenet in many philosophical and spiritual traditions. In the Bhagavad Gita, Lord Krishna advises Arjuna to focus on the work itself, not on its fruits. The teaching is clear: sincere action, performed without attachment to results, leads to inner peace. Buddhism emphasizes right livelihood and right effort as integral parts of the Eightfold Path toward enlightenment. Even in Christian theology, honest labor is considered a way to honor God and to cultivate virtues like patience, humility, and perseverance.

Modern psychology, too, echoes these ancient insights. Studies in positive psychology reveal that people who engage in "flow" activities — tasks that fully absorb their attention and challenge their skills — report higher levels of happiness and fulfillment. Flow arises naturally from sincere work, from a state where self-consciousness fades, and one becomes wholly immersed in the act of doing. Whether it is an artist lost in painting, a surgeon focused during an operation, or a teacher passionately engaged with students, the state of flow nourishes the human spirit and fosters enduring happiness.

Sincere work also has a transformative power. It refines character, builds resilience, and develops virtues that are essential for a meaningful life. Hardships encountered in sincere labor teach patience. Failures met with integrity strengthen humility. Perseverance in the face of obstacles cultivates courage. Over time, these qualities form the bedrock of a stable, contented mind — a mind less swayed by external circumstances and more anchored in inner peace.

The road to sincere work, however, is not always easy. It requires self-discipline to resist the temptations of shortcuts and easy gains. It demands courage to remain true to one's principles when faced with adversity. It calls for humility to accept that sincere work may not always be immediately rewarded or recognized. Yet, it is precisely these challenges that make the rewards so profound. The happiness born of overcoming obstacles through honest effort is deeper and more enduring than any happiness derived from luck or privilege.

Sincere work is intimately tied to the concept of purpose. When people find work that resonates with their sense of meaning, they are more likely to engage in it sincerely. Purpose transforms labor into a calling, into something larger than oneself. It connects daily toil with a vision of personal growth or service to others. The farmer who sees feeding people as his mission, the doctor who heals with compassion, the teacher who shapes young minds — each finds in their work a reservoir of meaning that nourishes their spirit and sustains their happiness.

At its core, sincere work requires the abandonment of ego. When work is done for recognition or validation, it becomes entangled with pride and fear. The sincere worker, however, does not seek applause or fear criticism. They work because the work itself is worthwhile.

They find joy not in the outcome, but in the process. Such detachment from ego liberates the mind, allowing it to find contentment in the simple act of doing. The worker becomes one with the work, and in that union, lasting happiness blooms.

In a society often obsessed with quick success and instant gratification, the value of sincere work is easily forgotten. People chase after titles, possessions, and accolades, believing them to be the keys to happiness. Yet, countless examples prove otherwise. Celebrities, billionaires, and public figures often struggle with dissatisfaction and inner turmoil despite their wealth and fame. True happiness, it seems, eludes even the most externally successful if their work lacks sincerity and inner alignment.

Conversely, many who live humble lives — artisans, teachers, farmers, caregivers — often exhibit a quiet, steady happiness born from the satisfaction of sincere labor. Their lives may not be adorned with riches or honors, but they are rich in meaning and contentment. They do not measure their worth by external standards but by the sincerity with which they live and work. Their happiness endures because it is rooted in something unshakable.

Sincere work also fosters connection — to others, to nature, and to the broader human story. Work done with honesty and dedication often serves others, builds communities, and preserves traditions. The weaver who creates cloth with care, the carpenter who builds homes with precision, the farmer who tends the earth with respect — each contributes to the tapestry of human life in ways that money or fame alone cannot measure. Through sincere work, individuals become part of something larger, and this sense of belonging nourishes the soul.

Moreover, sincere work is an antidote to existential despair. When life's inevitable sorrows — loss, failure, loneliness — arise, those who have devoted themselves to sincere work find solace and resilience. Their lives have been built upon solid ground. They have known the joy of creation, the discipline of effort, the humility of honest labor. These experiences fortify the spirit, making it less vulnerable to despair. Sincere work anchors life in meaning, and meaning, as Viktor Frankl observed, is the deepest wellspring of human happiness.

There is also a beauty to sincere work that transcends utility. It is an aesthetic experience, a form of art. A field well-plowed, a room carefully cleaned, a meal lovingly prepared — all speak of the human capacity to infuse even the simplest tasks with grace and dignity. Sincere work ennobles both the doer and the deed. It transforms the ordinary into the extraordinary, and in doing so, reveals the sacred hidden within the everyday.

Happiness that comes from sincere work is not loud or ostentatious. It is quiet, steady, and enduring. It does not depend on external validation or fluctuating fortunes. It is a happiness that can withstand the test of time, the trials of life, and the storms of fate. It is a happiness born not of what is achieved but of how it is achieved — with honesty, integrity, and wholehearted devotion.

In the final analysis, sincere work is not merely a path to lasting happiness; it is lasting happiness itself. It is the practice of living truthfully, acting authentically, and giving oneself fully to the task at hand. It is a way of aligning one's outer actions with one's inner values, creating a life that is both meaningful and joyful. It is the secret known to all great souls — that happiness is not something we find at the end of the road but something we cultivate with every sincere step along the way.

The world may tempt us with easier routes, with promises of quick success and effortless pleasure. But those who have walked the path of sincere work know otherwise. They understand that the deepest contentment comes not from what we receive but from what we become through honest labor. They know that a life built on sincerity is a life built on rock, not sand. They have tasted the quiet joy that comes from giving their best, from pouring themselves into their work without reservation. Thus, the enduring truth remains unmistakably clear: lasting happiness arises only from sincere awareness, honest reflection, and dedicated effort.

❐

Chapter-18

Creativity is one of the Biggest Symptoms of a Living Being, Happiness is Its Natural Outcome

Life is not merely the mechanical continuity of biological processes; it is a dynamic, self-expressive phenomenon. Across the grand canvas of existence, from the most primitive organisms to the most complex human civilizations, life has always expressed itself through creativity. It is creativity that differentiates the living from the non-living, the vibrant from the inert, the conscious from the unconscious. Creativity, in its purest form, is the deepest symptom of being alive, and happiness, quietly and inevitably, is its natural and most enduring outcome.

Every living being, in some measure, is creative. In the instinctual domain of animals, we see the creativity of survival — the bird weaving its nest, the spider spinning its web, the beaver constructing its dam. These are not random acts but intelligent, adaptive expressions of life. Even in the microscopic world, bacteria mutate and adapt, a form of biological creativity that ensures their survival. Life responds to challenges not with rigidity but with creative improvisation. It finds ways where there are none, expresses itself in forms unforeseen, and in doing so, asserts its living essence.

When life stops being creative, it stops thriving. A stagnant pond decays, a mind trapped in rigid thought shrivels, a society without innovation declines. Creativity is life's way of maintaining its freshness and resilience. It is the sign that a being is not merely existing but living — actively participating in the ongoing act of creation that is the universe itself.

For humans, creativity transcends biological necessity and becomes a profound act of self-expression. Beyond the realm of survival, humans build civilizations, compose music, paint, write poetry, invent machines, and discover scientific truths. These acts are not driven solely by need but by an intrinsic impulse to express, to know, to shape, and to participate in the mystery of existence. The child drawing on the walls, the poet lost in verses, the scientist pondering the cosmos, the artisan shaping clay — all are manifestations of this life-force seeking expression.

Creativity is not confined to the traditionally artistic domains. It is present wherever there is original thought, wherever life encounters obstacles and responds not with despair but with new possibilities. A teacher who finds a better way to explain a concept, a farmer experimenting with new cultivation methods, a doctor innovating in surgery — all these are acts of creativity. Creativity, therefore, is not the privilege of a few; it is the birthright of all who are truly alive.

The creative impulse arises from the inherent freedom of life. Unlike inanimate objects, which move according to fixed laws, living beings possess a degree of autonomy. They choose, they experiment, they learn. This autonomy, this freedom, is the soil in which creativity grows. It allows life to not merely adapt to circumstances but to imagine and create new ones.

In expressing creativity, life not only ensures its survival but also experiences its deepest joy. For creativity is not laborious drudgery; it is play. It is the spontaneous, joyful outpouring of inner vitality. The bird does not seem burdened when building its nest; the child at play is not struggling but rejoicing. In the very act of creation, there is a fulfillment that transcends external rewards. The creator, at the moment of creation, is complete, and happiness wells up naturally, effortlessly.

This happiness is not the shallow pleasure of distraction or consumption. It is not the fleeting thrill that fades with novelty. It is a profound, abiding happiness — the happiness of being true to one's nature, of participating in the creative flow of life. It is the happiness that arises when the self dissolves in the act, when the doer and the deed are one.

Psychologists call this state "flow" — a condition of deep engagement where the individual loses sense of time, self-consciousness fades, and pure immersion in the activity occurs. Flow is the hallmark of genuine creativity, and it is invariably accompanied by happiness. Studies have shown that people who regularly experience flow report higher levels of life satisfaction, greater emotional well-being, and deeper fulfillment. They are not necessarily the wealthiest or the most famous, but they are rich in the currency that matters most: inner joy.

Creativity also fosters growth. It challenges limits, breaks barriers, and expands horizons. The creative mind is never stagnant; it is always exploring, learning, evolving. In this continual expansion lies another secret of happiness. Growth is an intrinsic need of life. A plant must grow, a child must develop, a mind must mature. When growth is stifled, life withers; when it is nurtured, life flourishes. Creativity ensures growth, and growth ensures happiness.

Moreover, creativity connects the individual to the larger whole. Every act of creation, however small, is a participation in the grand creative process of the universe. The poet weaving words, the musician crafting melodies, the scientist unraveling mysteries — all are tapping into the same source that spins galaxies and blooms flowers. In creating, one feels less isolated, more connected to the vast web of life. This sense of connection, of being part of something larger than oneself, brings a deep and lasting happiness that mere individual achievement cannot.

Creativity also fosters resilience. Life is not without its trials, but the creative spirit sees in every challenge an opportunity to innovate, to adapt, to transcend. It transforms obstacles into stepping stones, wounds into wisdom, failures into new beginnings. This resilience, born of creativity, shields happiness against the tempests of fate. It makes happiness not a fragile gift dependent on circumstances, but a robust companion, sustained by the continual act of creative engagement with life.

At the societal level, creativity is the engine of progress. Every leap in human civilization — the discovery of fire, the invention of the wheel, the birth of democracy, the breakthroughs in science and technology — has been the fruit of creative minds daring to imagine the new. Societies that encourage creativity flourish; those that suppress it stagnate. A society rich in creative expression is vibrant, dynamic, and alive, and its people, engaged in meaningful and creative pursuits, experience greater happiness and fulfillment.

Yet creativity requires certain conditions to flourish. Freedom is essential — not the license to do anything, but the space to explore, to experiment, to fail, and to try again. Fear is the great enemy of creativity. Fear of failure, fear of judgment, fear of the unknown — these stifle the creative impulse. A culture that values conformity over originality, efficiency over exploration, control over curiosity, inadvertently suffocates the life-force itself.

To nurture creativity, both in individuals and societies, requires a shift in values — from mere productivity to meaningful engagement, from rigid certainty to open inquiry, from external validation to inner satisfaction. Education systems must encourage not just rote learning but critical thinking, imagination, and innovation. Workplaces must allow room for experimentation and original thought. Communities must celebrate not just success but effort, not just outcomes but sincere endeavor.

On a personal level, cultivating creativity requires courage — the courage to be vulnerable, to risk failure, to step into the unknown. It demands humility — the willingness to learn, to be wrong, to be surprised. It calls for patience — the understanding that creative growth is often slow, non-linear, and unpredictable. Most of all, it requires love — a deep, abiding love for life, for truth, for beauty, for the sheer joy of creation itself.

In the modern world, where distractions are many and attention is fragmented, nurturing creativity has become both more challenging and more necessary. The lure of passive consumption — endless entertainment, constant social media, superficial engagements — dulls the creative spirit. True creativity demands periods of silence, of solitude, of focused immersion. It requires a retreat from the noise to listen to the deeper rhythms within.

Those who make this space for creativity find not only greater happiness but a deeper sense of meaning. For creativity aligns one with the fundamental nature of life — to grow, to express, to evolve. It transforms existence from a series of mechanical routines into an ongoing act of creation, filled with wonder and possibility.

History is replete with individuals who have embodied this truth. Leonardo da Vinci, with his insatiable curiosity and boundless creativity, found joy not just in painting but in inventing, exploring anatomy, studying the flight of birds. Rabindranath Tagore, the great poet and polymath, expressed creativity in literature, music, art, and education, finding in each act a profound happiness. Albert Einstein spoke of the *"joy of thinking,"* a happiness rooted in the creative exploration of the mysteries of the universe.

These figures remind us that creativity is not a luxury or a hobby but the essence of a life fully lived. It is the bridge between the self and the world, the visible and the invisible, the known and the unknown. It is the song of life itself, and those who listen and respond to it find happiness not as a goal but as a natural accompaniment to the journey.

Creativity, ultimately, is the flowering of the soul. It is the outward expression of inner vitality, the dance of life in form and color and sound and thought. When we create, we affirm life; we participate in the ongoing miracle of existence. And in that affirmation, in that participation, happiness arises — not forced, not contrived, but as naturally as a flower blooms or a bird sings.

In the final analysis, creativity is the biggest symptom of a living being because it is life itself seeking expression. Happiness is its natural outcome because to create is to live fully, to engage wholly, to be present completely. Creativity and happiness are not separate pursuits but two sides of the same coin. To nurture one is to invite the other. A life that creates is a life that rejoices. A heart that dares to imagine, to build, to express, is a heart that knows true happiness. Thus, amid all the complexity of existence, this simple truth endures: creativity is the purest sign of life, and happiness is its most natural gift.

❐

Chapter-19

Seeds of Character, Roots of Change: The Critical Role of Evolution of the self in Children

Personality is not something that begins in adulthood. It is not a fixed trait we acquire later in life, nor is it shaped overnight by education or professional success. It begins to form the moment a child becomes aware of himself and the world around him. A child's personality is like soft clay—pliable, impressionable, and rich with potential. What adults offer during these foundational years—through love, guidance, structure, and freedom—becomes the shaping hand of their future self.

Raising a child, therefore, is not only about providing food, education, and safety. It is about nurturing the very essence of who they are. It is about building their self-confidence, helping them discover their voice, and guiding them to become emotionally strong, ethically grounded, and socially capable human beings. The foundations we lay in childhood echo across the entirety of life.

Every child has a unique inner world—a kaleidoscope of emotions, thoughts, and imagination. One of the earliest steps in evolution of self is allowing the child **to express themselves freely**. Whether they are talking, drawing, dancing, singing, or simply asking questions, their expressions must be received with openness and interest. When a child feels heard without judgment, they begin to trust their own thoughts and feelings. This trust becomes the seed of confidence.

Parents and teachers must **listen patiently, respond kindly, and allow space for individuality to bloom.** Correct them when needed, **but never ridicule.** A child who is comfortable expressing themselves will grow into an adult who can communicate clearly, connect with others, and remain emotionally healthy.

Children are like mirrors—they reflect what they see around them. If they grow up in an **environment of honesty, respect, kindness, and responsibility,** these qualities will quietly root themselves in their personality. Values are not best taught through lectures; they are absorbed through daily experiences, stories, and above all, the behavior of adults.

Tell children **tales of courage, integrity, and compassion**. Share examples of kindness, show appreciation for good deeds, and gently correct selfish behavior. Set rules, but explain why they matter. The earlier children are exposed to strong moral foundations, the more naturally they learn to make the right choices—not out of fear, but out of understanding.

Curiosity is the mother of learning. When children ask "Why?" or "How?", they are not being difficult—they are trying to make sense of the world. One of the most important aspects of developing personality is preserving and nurturing this natural curiosity.

Instead of dismissing questions with "Because I said so," take a moment to explain or explore the answer together. Let them experiment, build, dismantle, observe, and wonder. A curious mind becomes an intelligent, thoughtful, and creative mind. It also helps children develop independent thinking, which becomes a cornerstone of a strong and original personality.

While freedom is important for creativity, **discipline** is essential for strength of character. Children thrive on structure—not rigidity, but predictable rhythms that give their day a sense of balance. When children follow routines for study, play, meals, sleep, and screen time, they learn time management, self-control, and responsibility.

Discipline does not mean punishment—it means helping the child understand limits and choices. A child who learns the value of time, the importance of patience, and the satisfaction of completing tasks becomes someone others can trust and respect. These small habits, practiced daily, shape a personality that is dependable and resilient.

Physical movement is not just good for health; it is essential for emotional and social development. Sports, outdoor games, dancing, or even climbing trees—these are all forms of learning. Children develop coordination, stamina, and energy, but also teamwork, leadership, and the ability to handle failure.

Play is also a child's first language of emotional expression. In play, they act out what they can't yet verbalize. Encouraging active play helps children release stress, develop self-esteem, and stay emotionally balanced. A physically active child is not only healthier—they are happier and more confident, and it shows in their personality.

No personality can fully bloom without the ability to **communicate.** Help children learn the power of words—not only in speaking but also in listening. Encourage storytelling, discussions, sharing daily experiences, and reading aloud. Teach them to look into the eyes while talking, to wait their turn, to respect another's opinion.

Correct them gently if they interrupt or shout, but never shame them. Communication is a lifelong tool—for building relationships, solving problems, and expressing emotions. A child who learns to speak clearly and listen sincerely will stand tall in every room they enter.

Children are not meant to grow in isolation. **Peer interaction** helps children understand cooperation, empathy, leadership, and conflict resolution. Encourage playdates, team games, school events, or cultural gatherings where children interact with others of their age and even different age groups.

They may have disagreements or feel left out at times, but these are also learning opportunities. Guide them to express their feelings, to apologize, to forgive, and to include others. A socially developed child learns to navigate the world with ease and grows into a mature, emotionally intelligent adult.

Let children make choices—what to wear, which book to read, how to arrange their toys, or what color to paint. These decisions, though small, build a sense of agency. When a child feels that their opinion matters, their confidence soars. Don't rush to correct every mistake. Let them fall and figure things out—your support should be present but not smothering.

Encourage them to try solving small problems on their own. Ask questions like "What do you think we should do?" instead of giving quick solutions. Independent thinking leads to problem-solving skills, and this autonomy becomes a pillar of personality strength.

One of the most dangerous ideas a child can absorb is that only winning matters. While achievement has its place, it is effort, progress, and character that deserve more attention. Applaud your child for trying hard, for being kind, for improving—even if they did not come first.

This helps the child understand that value lies in the journey, not just the destination. It protects them from becoming arrogant in success or broken in failure. Children who grow up being praised for their effort and behavior are more emotionally secure and motivated than those only rewarded for results.

Perhaps the most important step of all is this—children learn by watching. No amount of lectures will teach honesty if they see lies. No story of kindness will be enough if they see anger and disrespect at home. If you want your child to develop a strong, compassionate, disciplined personality, live that example yourself.

Say sorry when you're wrong. Show calm in stressful moments. Speak respectfully to all people. Value time. Read books. Help others. The values you live every day will silently become the values they carry forever.

Evolution of self is not a syllabus with a final exam. It is a continuous nurturing of the heart, mind, and character. These ten steps are not boxes to be ticked—they are doors to be opened again and again, each time with more understanding and care.

Children are like blooming flowers—each with their own fragrance, color, and pace of growth. Your presence, patience, and participation in their journey is what makes the biggest difference. In helping a child grow into a kind, confident, and wise person, we do more than shape a personality—we shape the future of the world.

The development of a child's personality begins long before formal schooling. It begins with the first lessons taught not through textbooks, but through daily habits—such as how to wash hands, keep surroundings clean, eat mindfully, and maintain a tidy body and home. These early instructions in **health and hygiene** are not minor matters; they are the building blocks of character. They instill discipline, self-respect, and a sense of responsibility for one's own body and space—qualities that form the basis of a well-developed personality.

Health and hygiene habits are the first moral education a child receives. When a child is taught to brush teeth regularly, wash hands before eating, cover the mouth while coughing, or keep shoes in their proper place, they learn to respect not only themselves but also those around them. Such small habits gradually shape attention to detail, orderliness, and care for the collective environment—essential aspects of a conscientious personality.

If these lessons are ignored, a child may grow physically, but will lack the inner structure needed to build self-discipline, awareness, and social harmony. Hence, the very first step of evolution of self begins with a child's relationship with their own body and immediate environment.

The Need for Evolution of self in Early Life

The foundation of personality is laid in early childhood, when the mind is most impressionable. During this stage, children are not merely acquiring knowledge—they are forming the emotional, behavioral, and moral frameworks that will guide them for life. These formative years are crucial for instilling traits such as **self-confidence, empathy, resilience, responsibility, and curiosity**.

Children today are growing in a world of constant stimuli—screens, sounds, comparisons, and complexities. Without guided personality development, they risk becoming anxious, distracted, emotionally immature, or socially withdrawn. Intelligence alone cannot carry them through life. It is personality—how they face challenges, relate with others, manage emotions, and hold values—that determines their growth as individuals.

Just as seeds need soil, water, and sunlight to grow, children need emotional security, positive role models, and ethical guidance to become confident and compassionate adults. This is the urgent need of our time: to raise not just literate but **complete human beings.**

Some major steps required to develop personality of the children

1. Begin with Daily Habits and Discipline

Children learn discipline not from harsh commands but from structured routines. Fixed sleep hours, regular meals, and responsibilities like arranging their books or watering plants instill a quiet sense of self-governance. Repeating these actions daily, children internalize that personal care and tidiness are acts of self-respect.

2. Provide a Secure and Loving Environment

A child blossoms where they feel safe, heard, and accepted. Love does not mean indulgence—it means consistent care, boundaries, and attention. A secure environment gives the child courage to explore and develop individuality without fear of rejection or ridicule.

3. Model What You Want Them to Become

Children do not merely listen—they imitate. When parents speak respectfully, admit mistakes, read books, or express gratitude, children absorb these behaviors unconsciously. Role modeling is the most powerful method of teaching.

4. Encourage Expression and Reflection

Children must be encouraged to express their thoughts, fears, and feelings. Create spaces where they can speak freely—through art, writing, music, or open conversation. Emotional literacy allows them to manage impulses and grow in self-understanding.

5. Develop a Sense of Responsibility

Give children age-appropriate responsibilities—feeding a pet, packing their school bag, or setting the table. These small duties develop accountability and pride in work. The message is clear: your actions matter.

6. Introduce the Child to the World Beyond Themselves

Take them to parks, museums, markets, and public places where they can observe, ask questions, and interact with diversity. Expose them to nature, different cultures, and people who live differently. This broadens their worldview and reduces selfishness.

7. Impart Values through Stories and Conversations

Stories are a child's window to life's deepest truths. Folk tales, epics, and real-life accounts of kindness, courage, truth, and sacrifice leave lasting impressions. Discuss moral dilemmas and decisions, helping children reason through right and wrong.

8. Build Communication and Social Skills

Evolution of self is incomplete without the ability to express oneself clearly and listen empathetically. Encourage eye contact, polite greetings, gratitude, and assertiveness. Teach them that listening is as powerful as speaking.

9. Introduce Silence, Stillness, and Self-Observation

Children should learn to be comfortable without gadgets and noise. Encourage five minutes of silence, nature observation, or writing a thought journal. These habits nurture introspection and inner peace—rare treasures in today's restless world.

10. Limit Comparisons and Encourage Individuality

Each child is unique. Instead of comparing them with siblings or classmates, help them discover their personal strengths—be it in drawing, helping, dancing, or asking thoughtful questions. Personality thrives when nurtured, not measured.

The Lasting Impact of a Developed Personality

A child whose personality has been carefully and lovingly shaped becomes a beacon of possibility in the world. Their impact is visible across every field of life:

In academics, they become focused learners—motivated not by fear of failure but by curiosity and pride in learning.

In relationships, they are respectful and empathetic, able to cooperate, apologize, and forgive.

In adversity, they remain emotionally stable, showing courage, patience, and the ability to bounce back.

In leadership, they rise naturally—not by dominating others, but by inspiring trust and offering vision.

In character, they become ethical individuals, not easily tempted by dishonesty or shortcuts. They value integrity over applause.

In society, they grow into citizens who not only understand their rights but also honor their responsibilities.

Thus, the fruits of early evolution of self extend far beyond personal success—they shape a more humane, aware, and balanced society.

From Self to Society: Cultivating Civic Sense in Children

The final test of personality is not in how one behaves for personal gain, but in how one contributes to the collective good. This is where **civic sense** comes in—a vital part of personality often overlooked in childhood education. Civic sense includes awareness of public hygiene, respect for rules, care for the environment, and courtesy in shared spaces.

Teach children to throw trash in bins not because it is a rule, but because it protects beauty and health. Encourage them to keep noise levels down in public not because someone is watching, but because someone may be resting. Let them understand that waiting their turn, respecting traffic rules, or speaking kindly to domestic helpers are not just good manners—they are pillars of civil life.

When a child learns to **give back to society**, however small the gesture—planting a tree, helping an elderly neighbor, participating in a cleanliness drive—they feel a sense of belonging to something bigger than themselves. This is the highest stage of personality development: when self-respect matures into **social responsibility**.

In a time when individual success is worshipped, let us not forget the quiet heroism of a child who says thank you, closes the tap after use, and stands up for what is right. Such a child does not just have a personality—they have a soul awake to the needs of the world.

The journey of evolution of self in children begins with **teaching them to care for their body and surroundings** and culminates in **awakening their sense of civic duty**. Along the way, it shapes their identity, emotional landscape, communication skills, ethical clarity, and social consciousness.

To invest in a child's personality is to invest in a better world. It is a task that requires patience, presence, and purity of intent. But the reward is immeasurable: a generation that is not only smart, but wise; not only confident, but kind; not only ambitious, but just.

Let us then, as parents, teachers, and citizens, rise to this sacred task—not to control children, but to **liberate their fullest potential**. And let us begin with the small things: a hand washed, a word spoken kindly, a toy shared, a street kept clean. For in these simple acts, the future is being quietly shaped.

❐

Chapter-20

From Potential to Power: Guiding Teenagers to Master Themselves

The teenage years mark a critical phase in human development—a time filled with emotional turbulence, profound self-discovery, and immense potential. Evolution of self during adolescence is not merely a process of refining outward behavior or communication skills; it is a journey of nurturing the whole being—mind, body, and soul. A well-developed personality becomes the strongest and most enduring asset a young individual can carry into adulthood.

The journey begins with self-awareness and the formation of identity. Adolescents must be gently guided to understand who they truly are—beyond social labels or expectations. They should be encouraged to explore their interests, beliefs, emotional patterns, strengths, and weaknesses. Through honest self-reflection, they begin to form an internal compass that guides their actions, choices, and relationships. The question "Who am I?" must not be feared or ignored, but embraced with curiosity and courage.

Once the roots of identity are laid, adolescents must be taught the importance of setting personal goals and visualizing a life of purpose. A young mind thrives on vision. Setting goals—academic, personal, or social—not only inspires action but teaches accountability, direction, and perseverance. When teenagers imagine the kind of individual they wish to become, their motivation deepens, and their habits gradually begin to align with that imagined self.

Equally important is the development of emotional intelligence, a cornerstone of maturity. Adolescents experience sharp emotional highs and lows, often without knowing how to manage them. Teaching them to recognize their emotions, to empathize with others, and to regulate their reactions fosters resilience, social harmony, and internal stability. This can be achieved through journaling, open dialogue, and guided reflection. Emotional maturity makes their personalities gentle, stable, and capable of meaningful connection.

Communication plays a vital role in shaping one's personality. Adolescents should be encouraged to express their thoughts with clarity, listen with attentiveness, and engage in respectful conversations. Their confidence grows when they feel heard, and their relationships deepen when they truly listen. Activities like debates, storytelling, and theatre can serve as powerful tools in honing both verbal and non-verbal expression, enabling them to represent themselves with dignity in any setting.

But a beautiful personality, without discipline, risks being directionless. Adolescents must be taught the value of structure and consistency. The ability to manage time wisely, to stick to routines, and to delay gratification is what separates wishful thinking from real achievement. Simple daily habits—like making a study plan, avoiding procrastination, or maintaining regular sleep cycles—instill order, focus, and a sense of personal responsibility.

As their minds begin to blossom, adolescents should also be trained to think critically and make informed decisions. Instead of spoon-feeding answers, parents and educators should pose questions that encourage reasoning and independent thought. Adolescents must learn to examine situations, weigh consequences, and take responsibility for their actions. This habit of reflection not only sharpens intellect but builds character and integrity.

A confident personality is often the result of small victories. Adolescents should be given opportunities to participate in a variety of pursuits—academic contests, community service, sports, or creative arts. Every achievement, however minor, builds a sense of competence. Even failure, when handled wisely, becomes a stepping stone to growth. Constructive feedback and encouragement allow them to develop a self-assured, resilient, and optimistic personality.

Personal appearance and physical well-being, though sometimes overlooked, play an essential role in self-perception. Adolescents should be taught that personal hygiene, healthy posture, and neat attire are not superficial, but deeply linked to self-respect. A healthy body supports a vibrant mind, and a presentable appearance generates confidence. They must understand that how one presents oneself in the world often determines how the world responds in return.

In building a complete personality, moral values and social responsibility must not be neglected. Adolescents should be introduced to timeless principles such as honesty, compassion, respect, and justice. They must be encouraged to care for the environment, respect elders, and serve those in need. These values, once internalized, give direction to ambition and bring depth to personality. A person guided by ethics becomes dependable, trustworthy, and admirable.

Finally, adolescents should be inspired to embrace lifelong learning and the habit of reflection. They should be encouraged to read widely, observe mindfully, and adapt with humility. Personality is not a finished product but a living evolution. The habit of regularly questioning oneself, evaluating actions, and learning from experience keeps them grounded, aware, and wise. Such individuals not only grow in life but become a source of light for others.

The personality of an adolescent is like wet clay—sensitive, moldable, full of possibility. With thoughtful effort, compassionate guidance, and a nurturing environment, it can be shaped into something extraordinary. The ten dimensions discussed here are not merely about external behavior; they aim to awaken the core of a person, enabling them to stand tall in the world with self-respect, clarity, and compassion.

As parents, teachers, mentors, and members of society, we share a collective responsibility—not to dictate rules, but to create spaces for growth. When we empower adolescents with awareness, discipline, values, and vision, we are not just preparing them for a livelihood—we are preparing them for life itself.

Let us remember, the greatest investment in our future is not in machines or buildings, but in the silent flowering of a young personality becoming its best self.

Poverty is not merely the absence of material wealth—it often comes with a painful absence of encouragement, opportunity, and visibility. Yet, within even the humblest of circumstances, the human spirit longs to rise. For adolescents who grow up in poverty, the development of personality is not a cosmetic pursuit—it is the very foundation upon which they can construct a life of dignity, hope, and contribution.

The first and most urgent step in evolution of self for such adolescents is to help them rediscover their sense of self-worth. In a world that often measures value in money and appearance, they must be gently taught that their existence has meaning, and their life carries potential. They must learn to say with quiet conviction: "I matter." This inner recognition of dignity becomes the seed from which every other dimension of personality can grow.

Exposure to encouraging role models is essential. Many poor adolescents have never seen someone from their background achieve something noteworthy. Introducing them to real-life stories—of teachers, police officers, community leaders, soldiers, or scientists—who emerged from humble beginnings can ignite a powerful belief: *If they could do it, why not I?* Role models make aspirations real and reachable.

The next step is to help these young individuals understand the power of personal hygiene and neat appearance. Even in the absence of costly clothes or modern grooming products, a clean, well-maintained look radiates self-respect. Adolescents can be taught simple practices: daily bathing, clean nails, combed hair, and tidy clothes—even if limited in number. These efforts influence how others treat them and how they perceive themselves.

One of the most vital areas of evolution of self is communication. Adolescents from poor households often struggle with confidence in speech due to limited exposure. This can be changed through storytelling, role-playing, peer dialogue, and listening exercises. When a child learns to express thoughts clearly and respectfully, a quiet power enters their personality. They begin to feel seen and heard, which is the heart of personal growth.

Education remains the central pillar of transformation. For those who cannot afford coaching classes or expensive schools, the cultivation of self-study habits becomes critical. They can be taught how to use free resources—libraries, shared notes, group study, mobile apps—and how to structure their day around learning. The discipline of daily study builds confidence and a sense of control over one's future. It also nurtures the mind to think critically and dream freely.

But personality is not shaped by intellect alone—it is also forged in the fire of emotional experience. Poor adolescents are often exposed to stress, humiliation, or neglect. Without guidance, these experiences can fester into anger, fear, or helplessness. Therefore, emotional management must be taught through simple practices: breathing exercises, talking circles, writing journals, and teaching how to respond—not react—to life's provocations. The strength to remain calm amidst storms is one of the greatest achievements of personality development.

Time, unlike money, is equally distributed. Teaching adolescents to respect and utilize time is transformative. With just a pencil and paper, they can create daily timetables—balancing study, chores, rest, and leisure. When they begin planning their days, they begin owning their lives. Time discipline fosters seriousness, reduces wastage, and invites self-confidence. It prepares them to function with efficiency and responsibility.

Physical activity is another area that shapes the body and sharpens the character. Adolescents can be involved in sports, morning walks, group yoga, or simple community drives like tree planting or cleanliness campaigns. These actions not only improve health but also instill habits of teamwork, responsibility, and purposeful energy. A fit body often reflects a focused and motivated personality.

At the core of personality lies a moral compass. Values such as honesty, humility, kindness, and respect for others must be embedded in daily life. These values are not abstract—they are practiced in returning borrowed books, offering help to elders, speaking truth even when difficult, and learning to say thank you or sorry with sincerity. In a world that often values smartness over goodness, it is important to remind adolescents that character is the most lasting wealth they can own.

Finally, skill development adds a powerful dimension to personality. Acquiring a practical skill—be it stitching, painting, mobile repairing, farming techniques, or computer basics—gives adolescents a sense of economic possibility. Earning even a small amount through their own skill brings them pride, independence, and recognition. These experiences uplift posture, sharpen purpose, and add a glow of dignity to their personality.

In conclusion, evolution of self for poor adolescents is not a supplementary project; it is a social necessity. When nurtured with compassion, structure, and encouragement, these young lives blossom—not just into better individuals but into sources of inspiration for others. Their journey from neglect to self-respect is a story worth investing in—for their sake, and for the future of society.

❒

Chapter-21

It's Never too Late: Empowering Adults to Grow Beyond Limits

At the summit of one's career, when the applause resounds, the accolades pile up, and the responsibilities tower higher than ever, it is easy to believe that the journey of evolution of self has reached its completion. But this illusion is far from the truth. In fact, the peak is not the end of the journey—it is a delicate turning point. The air at the top is thin, and survival requires more than the skills and drive that got one there; it demands inner refinement, emotional intelligence, and vision that transcends personal ambition.

Evolution of self at this stage becomes an inward journey—subtler, deeper, and more meaningful than ever before. To begin, one must start with sincere self-reflection. When all titles, posts, and designations are stripped away, what remains? The individual at the height of a profession must ask: Who am I beyond the nameplate on the door or the respect of subordinates? This stage requires peeling away the external accolades and engaging with the core identity. Self-awareness now becomes not a tool for ascent, but a mirror for truth. With such clarity comes the realization that the journey is not merely about status, but about contribution.

As roles expand and impact multiplies, the need to define or even redefine one's purpose arises. While in earlier years, success might have been driven by aspiration, now the question is of meaning. What do I stand for? What will I leave behind? A matured personality at this phase begins to orbit around legacy—not in terms of wealth or fame, but in the quiet, lasting difference made to individuals, systems, and society.

However, with position often comes power, and with power, the subtle dangers of pride, restlessness, and emotional imbalance. Therefore, mastering emotional regulation becomes indispensable. A person at the top will often face situations where envy, frustration, or unchecked authority may distort judgment. A developed personality is not reactive but composed—anchored in calm discernment. This does not mean absence of emotion, but control over its expression. One learns to respond, not react.

In the same vein, listening emerges as a critical yet underestimated skill. Ironically, the more powerful a person becomes, the less honest feedback they receive. People hesitate, soften criticism, or flatter. The evolved individual trains themselves to listen actively and sincerely—not only to what is being said, but also to what is not being spoken.

Listening with attention and empathy deepens insight and sustains healthy relationships with colleagues, juniors, and even adversaries.

At this altitude, humility is not an ornament; it is oxygen. The great leaders and professionals are remembered not only for their achievements, but for the way they made others feel. A graceful acknowledgment of the team's effort, a public word of gratitude to one's mentors, and private moments of sincere humility—these small gestures add profound depth to the personality. The proud may command obedience, but the humble win respect.

Yet humility does not mean passivity. The truly evolved personality keeps learning—more so than before. One reads not for exams or promotions but for insight. One attends events not for visibility but for evolution. Staying open to learning from juniors, from other fields, from one's own mistakes—this is a rare trait at the top, but the most necessary. Growth must become lifelong. The day one believes there is nothing left to learn is the day personality stops growing and begins to decline.

Another important shift at this stage is the disidentification with one's title. To evolve further, a person must detach their self-worth from their professional designation. They are not merely a director, general, judge, or CEO—they are a human being with values, emotions, and a mind. This separation allows inner freedom. It makes the individual resilient against the shocks of retirement, replacement, or societal transitions.

Simultaneously, attention must be redirected to the body. A peak position often extracts a toll on health through irregular schedules, stress, or neglect. But now the body must be seen as a sacred vehicle. Health is no longer a lifestyle choice; it is a responsibility. One must embrace fitness, sound sleep, clean eating, and preventive care—not just for personal benefit, but as an example to others. Without physical vitality, even the sharpest intellect fades.

Equally, emotional wellness demands that one nurture genuine social bonds. Beyond formal networks and strategic relationships, the soul craves authentic friendships. At this juncture, reconnecting with childhood companions, family members, or forming new bonds without expectations can ground the personality. The top is lonely only for those who fail to build bridges of warmth.

In parallel, the truly developed personality now begins to promote others. Empowering younger colleagues, nurturing talent, and stepping back from limelight to let others shine is not weakness—it is greatness. One's worth is no longer measured by dominance, but by the leaders one helps shape. Mentorship becomes a mode of influence and joy.

With growing visibility, criticism also becomes inevitable. Some will find faults. Some will disagree. The emotionally mature person at the peak handles this with grace. They listen, accept what is valid, ignore what is untrue, and never take it personally. This attitude of learning from criticism reflects deep inner security. It shows a strength beyond defensiveness.

An essential skill now is the ability to use time wisely. Earlier, time was a resource to be maximized. Now it is a sacred flow to be respected. Not every meeting needs to be attended. Not every invitation needs a yes. The evolved personality chooses quality over quantity. Time is invested in causes, relationships, and pursuits that bring inner fulfillment—not merely external applause.

Closely connected to this is the need to detach from constant validation. Social media likes, public praise, and official honors no longer determine happiness. The true joy lies in the silent satisfaction of good work done with integrity. When one's sense of worth becomes internal, personality gains great stability.

At this maturity of life and profession, spirituality assumes greater importance. This may or may not be religious. But a daily inner pause, a prayer, meditation, or a walk in nature becomes essential. The developed personality accepts life's uncertainties, success and failure, applause and silence—with a deep sense of equanimity. Spiritual depth ensures the continuity of grace even in moments of loss.

And from this spiritual foundation emerges a natural urge to give back. The seasoned individual now seeks to support causes, contribute to society, and uplift the underprivileged. This is not charity—it is character. Whether through donations, volunteering, or knowledge-sharing, the act of giving completes the circle of receiving. The giver becomes the richest soul.

In these twilight years of a career, the individual must strengthen their ethical compass. When others bend rules for comfort or gain, the developed personality stands firm. Integrity is not negotiable. It is not an act but a state of being. Every ethical decision taken in private reflects and reinforces the strength of personality in public.

And as the time comes closer to handing over the mantle, a wise person prepares for succession. Not with fear, but with foresight. They train, guide, and bless their successors. They welcome fresh energy without insecurity. They understand that continuity is greater than control. In doing so, they ensure that their work lives on through others.

Finally, there comes the time to accept change. To embrace retirement, physical slowing down, or reduced visibility—not as decline, but as evolution. There is dignity in stepping back. There is peace in letting go. There is beauty in becoming a silent pillar instead of a loud torchbearer. Acceptance of impermanence is the crown jewel of personality.

And as the curtain of the professional journey begins to lower, the truly developed person does not retreat in silence. They write, speak, or share their experiences. They convert lessons into legacies. Their stories inspire generations. They live on—not in buildings named after them—but in the courage, character, and conduct of those they touched.

In the final analysis, evolution of self at the peak is not about adding layers but about shedding illusions. It is not about climbing higher, but about going deeper. It is about transforming from a high-achiever into a wise, grounded, graceful human being—one whose presence brings value, whose silence speaks volumes, and whose departure leaves behind a light that others can follow.

❐

Chapter-22
Beyond the Finish Line: The True Journey of Self Begins Now

Retirement marks a profound shift in one's life journey. It is not merely a cessation of employment or a farewell to the workplace; it is an invitation to rediscover the self beyond roles and responsibilities. For decades, a person's identity often becomes synonymous with their profession—be it a teacher, doctor, officer, or executive. However, once the office doors close and the official duties fade into memory, a new chapter begins—a chapter that calls not for rest alone, but for rejuvenation, reflection, and inner refinement.

The years after retirement can be the most meaningful if approached not with a sense of loss, but with a sense of liberation. Evolution of self in this phase is about rediscovering identity, cultivating peace, engaging meaningfully with the world, and preparing oneself for a graceful conclusion of life's journey. Here is a step-by-step pathway for evolution of self after retirement—a journey from external achievement to internal fulfillment.

The first and perhaps most important step is to accept retirement not as an end but as a new beginning. Society often views retirement with a sense of closure, as though one's relevance has expired. But in truth, retirement offers the precious gift of time—time to be, to reflect, to give back, and to evolve. When viewed through this lens, retirement becomes a second birth—one where the roles are self-chosen, the tasks are soulful, and the rewards are inner.

With this acceptance must come a reconstruction of identity. After decades of being known as "Sir," "Madam," or "Doctor," it is essential to see oneself beyond professional labels. Titles fade, but the individual remains. A retired person must consciously detach from designations and ask, "Who am I without my position?" This question does not lead to emptiness—it leads to freedom. It creates space for a more authentic self to emerge.

Having accepted change and reclaimed identity, the next movement is inward—to revisit one's purpose. Earlier, life may have revolved around deadlines, family needs, and professional aspirations. Now, it is time to redefine purpose in terms of contribution, legacy, and inner peace. Whether it is mentoring youth, engaging in creative pursuits, serving a cause, or simply spreading love in the family—this stage demands a purpose rooted in values, not ambition.

In this process of renewal, emotional cleansing becomes vital. Retirement can leave behind residues of regret—unfulfilled goals, bitter workplace memories, strained relationships, or lost opportunities. These emotional weights must be acknowledged, processed, and released. Forgiveness becomes a powerful tool—not just towards others, but towards oneself. Personality cannot evolve unless the heart is unburdened.

With emotional balance established, it becomes essential to create new routines and rhythms. The structure once provided by work must now be self-designed. Days should not be allowed to drift aimlessly. A balanced daily schedule—integrating physical exercise, reading, prayer or reflection, creative work, and social interaction—brings a sense of continuity and purpose. When the body, mind, and spirit are given dedicated time, personality becomes holistic.

Physical activity deserves special emphasis in this phase. The body may be aging, but movement is still medicine. Regular walks, yoga, light aerobics, or even gardening keeps the muscles engaged and the spirit energized. A person who remains physically active maintains not only health but also dignity and confidence.

Parallel to bodily care is the nourishment of the mind. Retirement does not mean the end of learning—it is the beginning of voluntary, joyous, curiosity-led education. Whether it is reading books, attending lectures, watching documentaries, or exploring new fields of interest—lifelong learning keeps the personality intellectually alive and relevant. A retired mind is not old; a stagnant mind is.

Beyond solitary pursuits, the emotional richness of life depends greatly on relationships. In the rush of professional life, many relationships get neglected. Retirement offers a golden opportunity to reconnect—with a spouse who shared the journey silently, with children who once sought your attention, with old friends whose laughter once lit up your youth. Emotional availability, time, and shared moments now become your greatest gifts to loved ones.

While personal relationships deepen the private sphere, involvement in community creates meaning in the social sphere. Joining senior citizen forums, local cultural or literary groups, spiritual gatherings, or NGOs reweaves the social fabric. It provides stimulation, relevance, and joy. Moreover, it prevents the isolation that many retirees silently endure. In being socially active, the personality expands beyond the home.

An extension of this engagement is the role of mentorship. There are countless young people in need of guidance—students preparing for careers, professionals facing dilemmas, or simply youth looking for role models. Retired individuals carry decades of distilled wisdom. Sharing this with humility and affection not only benefits others but makes the retired person feel truly purposeful. A mentor's personality radiates warmth and quiet authority.

Writing or journaling offers another profound avenue for self-expression. Whether it is memoirs, philosophical musings, poetry, or simple reflections on life, putting pen to paper clarifies the mind and heals the heart. It also creates a legacy—something tangible that can inspire others long after the writer is gone. In words, the personality finds permanence.

Along this path, the role of spirituality becomes increasingly prominent. This does not necessarily imply religious rituals. It means going inward. Whether through meditation, chanting, philosophical reading, or simply silent contemplation, spirituality lends depth and calm. It teaches acceptance, reduces fear of aging, and connects the individual to something larger than the ego. A spiritual personality is serene and wise.

In embracing spiritual simplicity, one is naturally drawn toward decluttering—both physical and mental. A simplified lifestyle, free from hoarding, unnecessary expenses, or constant craving, creates a sense of peace. The fewer the possessions, the freer the mind. When selfish desire s reduce, contentment increases. This simplicity reflects maturity and grace in personality.

To prevent the mind from falling into inertia, a new hobby or passion must be embraced. It could be painting, music, travel, learning a language, or photography. Retirement offers a second chance at forgotten dreams. Hobbies awaken creativity and joy, bringing childlike enthusiasm into a mature soul. A personality that retains playfulness never grows old.

However, even with all this joy, one must accept the natural changes of aging. The body will slow, memory may falter, energy may dip. Instead of resisting or resenting it, the developed personality accepts aging with dignity. Instead of trying to remain what they were, the wise individual becomes who they are—gentle, reflective, compassionate. This acceptance is the hallmark of inner development.

Such a personality becomes a model of calmness and kindness. They do not seek to dominate conversations or impose opinions. Their presence itself soothes others. Their advice is gentle, their tone respectful, their actions thoughtful. They are neither loud nor passive—they are influential through subtlety.

One potential trap to avoid is over-controlling family dynamics. A retired person must resist the urge to micromanage their children or grandchildren. While wisdom is welcome, interference is resented. Supporting without suffocating, suggesting without insisting—this balance preserves relationships and dignity. A truly evolved personality respects boundaries.

With energy and time at hand, it becomes important to engage in causes larger than the self. Whether it is environmental conservation, animal care, education of underprivileged children, or spiritual service—contributing to a cause elevates the personality. It transforms the retiree into a giver, a server, a protector of values.

As life nears its final chapters, mental preparation for detachment becomes essential. Death is not a subject to be feared or denied—it is to be understood. Meditation on impermanence, reading of spiritual texts, and conversations about legacy help a person prepare peacefully. The developed personality does not run from death—it embraces life more deeply because of that awareness.

And finally, as all duties are fulfilled, as all chapters are written, the retiree must live in gratitude and grace. Every breath, every relationship, every sunrise must be received with wonder. Gratitude becomes the crown jewel of the personality. It is not about having everything—but about honoring everything one has received.

In the end, evolution of self after retirement is not a matter of technique—it is a matter of attitude. It is a transition from noise to silence, from action to reflection, from accumulation to contribution. The most beautiful personalities in the world are not always in power—they are often found in the humble homes of wise retirees who live with peace, give with joy, and leave the world with grace.

❒

Chapter-23
Fostering Personal Growth Among Organizational Functionaries

In a world that rewards speed, clarity, and consistent output, the capacity to work efficiently has become a necessity rather than a choice. Whether in professional settings, educational pursuits, household responsibilities, or personal aspirations, the quality of efficiency determines the success, timeliness, and meaningfulness of our efforts. Efficient work is not just about completing tasks quickly; it is about achieving goals with precision, purpose, and the optimal use of time and resources. It is about minimizing wastage—of energy, materials, thought, and moments—while maximizing impact and satisfaction. It is about doing the right work in the right way, at the right time.

The first essential requirement for getting work done efficiently is to be absolutely clear about the objective. No amount of energy or enthusiasm can substitute for a well-defined purpose. If one is unsure of what needs to be accomplished, the work is likely to become scattered, delayed, or completely misdirected. A clear objective sharpens focus, aligns intentions, and directs the course of action. It eliminates confusion and provides a reference point against which progress and completion can be measured. Clarity breeds commitment, and commitment fuels efficiency.

Once the objective is known, the second logical step is to break down the work into smaller, manageable tasks. This process of segmentation helps simplify complex undertakings and enables structured thinking. It also prevents the overwhelming feeling that often comes with large responsibilities. When a goal is broken into smaller parts, each part becomes easier to understand, execute, and track. The human mind can concentrate better on small units of work, and small successes along the way build momentum and confidence. For instance, if one has to organize a large event, breaking it into parts such as booking the venue, inviting participants, arranging logistics, and managing publicity makes the process less intimidating and more doable.

After the work has been divided into components, one must decide the order in which these components should be addressed. This is the art of prioritization. Some tasks are urgent, some are important, some are both, and some are neither. Not every task deserves equal attention or immediate action. Efficient individuals recognize the difference between what is essential and what is simply urgent. They learn to say no to low-value tasks and reserve their best energy for the highest-priority responsibilities. Prioritizing well avoids unnecessary delays, reduces distractions, and ensures that critical elements are addressed first. Prioritization requires judgment, and with experience, this judgment becomes sharper.

Along with prioritization, it is necessary to identify and allocate the resources required to carry out each task. Resources may include time, tools, manpower, materials, information, or financial support. Without adequate resources, even the best plans can falter. Efficient execution requires anticipating needs in advance and making sure they are in place. Moreover, wise resource allocation ensures that there is no overuse or underutilization. When resources are scarce, creativity and adaptability become important to use what is available in the most productive way. Successful people often distinguish themselves not by having more but by managing better what they have.

Having resources is not enough unless one also manages time well. Every task needs a realistic and thoughtfully structured timeline. A deadline creates urgency and a sense of responsibility. Time-bound goals discourage procrastination and help keep distractions at bay. Efficient work thrives on disciplined time use. If a task is long or complex, dividing it into phases or milestones helps in maintaining consistency and evaluating progress along the way.

A written schedule or digital planner can guide daily actions. While setting a timeline, one should also allow for minor disruptions and build in some buffer time. This protects the schedule from being derailed by unforeseen problems without making it too loose to lose momentum.

An often ignored but highly critical step in working efficiently is preparing the environment for work. Even the most focused mind can be pulled away by unnecessary interruptions, cluttered surroundings, or the absence of essential tools. Before beginning, one must organize the workspace, keep all required materials nearby, turn off irrelevant notifications, and mentally enter a zone of seriousness. Just like a stage must be set before the actors perform, an environment conducive to work sets the tone for meaningful action. A clean, quiet, and well-lit space is not just about comfort—it is about psychological readiness and enhanced concentration.

Once the setting is ready, the real work begins. This is the stage of focused and committed action. Efficiency does not emerge from half-hearted or distracted efforts. It comes from deep attention, consistent pace, and the avoidance of unnecessary multitasking. Doing one thing with full attention is always better than doing three things badly at once. Some prefer techniques like the Pomodoro method, where one works in short, intense intervals followed by small breaks. Others may choose longer uninterrupted periods of concentration. Whatever the style, the essence remains the same: when it's time to work, just work. Eliminate doubts, delay, and diversions.

As the work progresses, it becomes important to monitor the pace and direction. Constant self-checking ensures that one remains on course and catches mistakes early. Monitoring allows for minor corrections without needing a complete rework later. But one must also be flexible. Not all plans unfold exactly as expected. New challenges, better ideas, or changed circumstances may require one to revise the method or shift priorities. Efficiency is not rigid. It is adaptive. It involves holding on to the goal but being open about the path. Those who work with a flexible mindset are better prepared to overcome obstacles and seize opportunities.

Upon completing the core work, one must not rush to finish. The review phase is critical. This is where the work is tested for quality, consistency, and completeness. Reviewing helps detect gaps, refine the presentation, and enhance the final outcome. It is the difference between average and excellent output. Many times, a little extra time spent on editing, polishing, or clarifying can make the work significantly more impactful. Reviewing also allows one to view the work from the receiver's perspective—whether it's a reader, listener, viewer, or client. Good work must not only be done well but also be understood and appreciated well.

Finally, after the task is done and reviewed, take a few minutes to reflect. Reflection is not about repeating the task but about learning from it. What went right? What could have been avoided? Where did you save time, and where did you lose it? What can be done better next time? This self-evaluation becomes the seed for future growth. With each task, the person becomes more capable, more alert, and more efficient. Learning from one's own work is the hallmark of a developing personality. The road to mastery is paved not with repetition alone but with thoughtful repetition that evolves.

Efficient work is not the result of chance, talent, or pressure. It is the outcome of a cultivated mindset and a disciplined approach. The ten steps outlined above—clarifying the goal, breaking it into smaller tasks, prioritizing, gathering resources, setting timelines, organizing the environment, taking focused action, monitoring and adjusting, reviewing the outcome, and reflecting upon the process—form an integrated method. When practiced regularly, these steps do not remain mechanical—they become habits of thought and action. They become a part of character.

In truth, efficiency is a way of living with purpose and balance. It respects time, honors commitment, and brings peace. Efficient individuals do not just finish their work—they uplift the standard of their work and inspire others. They find joy in action and dignity in detail. They are not merely fast—they are thoughtful, steady, and impactful. In a world that often confuses busyness with productivity, true efficiency stands out as clarity in motion, discipline in practice, and excellence in result.

Whether you are a student, a professional, a homemaker, or an entrepreneur, these steps can empower you to complete your work with a sense of achievement and calm. Efficiency is not a trait we are born with—it is a capacity we build, step by step, with awareness, commitment, and learning. And once it becomes part of our nature, it transforms not only the way we work but the way we live.

❐

Chapter-24
Enhancing the Personal Growth of Functionaries Working at Lower Levels

In every organization—be it a government office, corporate firm, school, hospital, or law enforcement agency—the strength and success of the system depend not only on visionary leadership but equally on the discipline, diligence, and dependability of lower-level officials. These are the individuals who carry out the groundwork, implement plans, maintain records, handle equipment, and ensure that policies and decisions are translated into action. A chain is only as strong as its weakest link, and therefore, the efficiency and integrity of lower-level personnel determine whether the machine of governance or service delivery functions smoothly or falters. This article outlines ten systematic steps through which a lower-level official can deliver consistent, high-quality results and earn respect within the team and organization.

The first and most essential step is to understand one's role and responsibilities with absolute clarity. A lower-level official must not only know what tasks are assigned but also why those tasks matter in the larger scheme of things. This understanding helps in bringing purpose to everyday work. Whether it is maintaining records, managing files, inspecting documents, or assisting seniors, one must be aware of one's duties, reporting hierarchy, deadlines, and performance expectations. If there is any doubt, the official must proactively seek clarification from a superior rather than proceeding with incomplete understanding, which could lead to errors or mismanagement.

Once the responsibilities are clear, the next step is to follow instructions accurately and promptly. A good lower-level official does not take instructions lightly or casually. Whether the directive is verbal or written, it should be received attentively, noted down if necessary, and executed exactly as intended. This is where discipline in listening and reading becomes vital. If any instruction seems ambiguous or if practical difficulties arise in executing it, one must have the courage and sincerity to respectfully ask questions or report the problem before proceeding blindly. Following instructions without deviation is a mark of professional maturity and reliability.

After understanding and receiving instructions, the third step is to organize the day-to-day work methodically. Time and resource management are not only for top managers. Even a clerk in a public office or a junior technician in a factory must know how to plan his day. A checklist of tasks, prioritization of urgent work, and avoidance of distractions go a long way in boosting productivity. A well-organized desk, well-arranged files, and a clean working space may look like small things but they directly influence the efficiency and impression of an official. A disorganized environment often reflects a disorganized mind.

Punctuality and consistency form the fourth cornerstone of successful execution. A lower-level official must adhere to the work schedule, come on time, and ensure that tasks are not delayed due to personal inefficiency. A few minutes lost every day may appear insignificant, but they compound into large delays in the long run. Moreover, consistency builds reliability. When superiors and colleagues know that a particular official always delivers work on time, they begin to trust and depend on him more, which eventually opens doors for higher responsibilities and career progression.

The fifth step toward delivering good results is to report progress honestly and in a timely manner. Many tasks at the lower level are interlinked with other departments or superiors. If an official completes a file entry, verification, or inspection, it must be communicated to the next authority without delay. Equally important is the courage to report delays or mistakes early, rather than hiding them. Honest reporting not only prevents damage to the organization but also reflects the character of the official. A responsible attitude strengthens trust in the chain of command.

Learning and upgrading skills is the sixth systematic step. Just because a person occupies a lower post does not mean learning should stop. The workplace is a living classroom. A peon observing the filing system can learn data management. A lab assistant helping in reports can improve computer proficiency. A constable on the beat can develop observation and conflict-resolution skills. One must remain curious, open to learning from seniors, and even learn from one's own errors. Those who keep sharpening their tools are the ones who remain relevant and valuable in changing environments.

Team spirit and cooperative behavior constitute the seventh step in the journey toward excellence. An efficient official must work in harmony with colleagues, not in competition. Helping others when possible, avoiding unnecessary arguments, respecting differences, and contributing to a positive work environment creates a culture of trust. Even during stressful times, politeness and patience matter. A lower-level official who is friendly, dependable, and non-confrontational becomes a pillar of strength in any team.

The eighth step is handling resources, tools, and records with a sense of responsibility. A significant portion of lower-level work involves physical tasks—operating machines, handling files, maintaining logbooks, or issuing items. This requires alertness, caution, and care. Mishandling resources can lead to damage, delay, or financial loss to the organization. Records must be updated truthfully, and tools must be used properly and returned on time. Responsibility here is not limited to physical safety but extends to data integrity and procedural accuracy as well.

The ninth step is strict adherence to rules, ethics, and codes of conduct. Lower-level officials are often the face of the organization to the public. A receptionist, police constable, or hospital attendant interacts directly with people and therefore represents the dignity and discipline of the department. Taking bribes, leaking information, violating protocols, or behaving rudely tarnishes not just the individual but the whole system. Ethics must become second nature. Small dishonesties or neglect may go unnoticed initially, but in the long run, they destroy reputation and invite punishment.

Finally, the tenth and most empowering step is to take responsibility and show initiative. While following orders is the basic requirement, going beyond them when necessary shows leadership potential. If a pending task needs urgent attention, take the lead. If a superior forgets a deadline, gently remind them. If a process can be made more efficient, suggest it respectfully. Never say "this is not my job" for work that benefits the team. Initiative adds value to your role, and responsibility builds self-respect.

In conclusion, lower-level officials are the foundation upon which every administrative and organizational structure stands. Their punctuality, dedication, communication, and discipline directly influence whether the team succeeds or falters. By following the ten systematic steps described above—understanding responsibilities, obeying instructions, organizing work, being punctual, reporting progress, learning continuously, working cooperatively, handling tools responsibly, following ethical codes, and taking initiative—any lower-level official can transform their position into one of excellence and respect. Good results are not a matter of position or power; they are a reflection of how sincerely, systematically, and consistently we do our work, however small it may appear.

❐

Chapter-25

Enhancing Personal Growth of Mid-Level Executives in An Organization

A middle-level official occupies a pivotal position in any organization. Neither at the apex of power nor at the base of direct implementation, this role serves as the crucial link that transforms vision into action and strategy into results. The strength of any team, department, or institution depends significantly on how effectively its middle management functions. When leadership outlines a goal, it is the responsibility of the middle-level official to receive, interpret, break down, communicate, monitor, support, and ensure that it becomes a visible and measurable reality on the ground. This article presents, in narrative and integrated form, ten systematic practices through which a middle-level official can consistently generate good results and earn respect across the hierarchy.

The very first requirement for success in this role is to clearly understand the vision and intent of the leadership. The goals of the organization, its mission statements, targets, and timelines are not just to be acknowledged; they are to be deeply comprehended and interpreted in the practical language of the field or department. This means identifying what exactly the leadership wants and why, and then thinking through how that can be translated into practical, sequential steps that the working staff can implement. Once the vision is understood, the middle-level officer becomes the translator of that vision into the language of action.

This leads to the second requirement—breaking down large goals into smaller, specific assignments that match the skills, capacities, and current workload of the available personnel. Good work delegation is not simply about assigning work randomly or equally—it is about assigning work wisely. A capable middle-level official maps out who is strong in what, who needs support, and who is under or overburdened. By ensuring clarity in instructions and expected outcomes, confusion is reduced and accountability is created. Every subordinate must know not just what to do but also by when and in what format the results are to be presented.

Effective execution is possible only when communication flows efficiently. At the middle level, one must become the artery through which both upward and downward information travels reliably and accurately. This means not only listening carefully to the instructions of superiors and communicating them clearly to juniors, but also collecting ground-level feedback, concerns, and difficulties and conveying them upward with honesty and precision. In addition to formal reporting systems, informal conversations, team huddles, and open-door approaches become tools to ensure that no one feels left out or unheard. At the same time, records must be maintained for transparency and future reference.

Monitoring progress is not just about supervising others or policing behavior. It is a dynamic process that requires awareness, alertness, and flexibility. A good middle-level official keeps track of work not only through scheduled review meetings or written reports but also through unannounced observations, feedback from different sources, and his or her own intuition developed through experience. Delays, errors, bottlenecks, or poor coordination are inevitable in any system. The difference lies in identifying them early, understanding their root cause, and adapting strategy accordingly—whether by shifting resources, changing sequence, or reassigning roles. Correction at the right moment prevents crisis later.

Not all problems need to travel up the chain of command. In fact, a sign of a competent middle manager is his or her ability to resolve as many issues as possible at their own level. Whether the problem is related to a machine, a misunderstanding between staff, an ambiguous rule, or an administrative lapse, the officer must apply logic, experience, and emotional intelligence to address it efficiently. Only when the problem exceeds one's authority or technical understanding should it be escalated, and even then, it should be accompanied by a brief background and at least one recommended solution. This habit not only shows initiative but also earns the respect of superiors.

Middle-level officials are not only task managers; they are also people managers. It is vital to maintain the morale, motivation, and confidence of the team. When a subordinate performs well, timely appreciation and encouragement go a long way in reinforcing good behavior. When someone is struggling, guidance must be provided patiently. Motivation is not a one-time event; it is a continuous process of communication, presence, and support. Being available for your team, asking about their challenges, and helping them overcome small setbacks creates a work environment where people feel safe and inspired to give their best. Constructive feedback and mentoring convert average workers into valuable assets.

No team can succeed without discipline and order. It is the responsibility of the middle-level official to ensure that there is consistency in timelines, procedures, and record-keeping. Deadlines must be respected and enforced. All documentation—from leave registers and progress charts to performance logs and correspondence—must be updated accurately and on time. Delays or negligence at this level create a ripple effect that may disturb the entire system. Therefore, this role requires not only self-discipline but also the ability to instill the same in others. Setting an example through punctuality, consistency, and neatness in work habits influences the team more than words alone can.

Often, the success of one department is tied to coordination with others. Middle-level officials must actively engage in building professional relationships across departments, wings, or units. Whether it's seeking timely approval, requesting a resource, or clarifying a procedural issue, the ability to navigate inter-departmental boundaries with cooperation, tact, and firmness is a defining skill. Misunderstandings, blame games, and territorial attitudes can derail even the best internal functioning. It is the middle-level official who can act as the bridge that connects different parts of the system and enables smooth functioning through trust and mutual respect.

Leaders often rely on middle-level officials for ground realities. Therefore, the way reports and data are presented becomes crucial. An honest, well-structured, and timely report not only conveys the current status but also helps senior officers take informed decisions. A report that hides problems or exaggerates achievements may create short-term comfort but leads to long-term failure. Presenting both accomplishments and concerns with balance and clarity demonstrates maturity and builds credibility. Timely escalation of red flags helps prevent disasters and also positions the official as dependable and forward-thinking.

Finally, no matter how competent an officer becomes, the journey of improvement must never stop. Every assignment offers lessons—about people, processes, and systems. Reflecting on these lessons, being open to feedback from juniors as well as seniors, and welcoming new ideas keep the work culture fresh and adaptive. Encouraging the team to learn, propose innovations, and seek efficiency improvements creates a dynamic rather than a stagnant environment. Upskilling, whether through formal training or self-learning, ensures readiness for higher responsibilities and enhances the overall performance of the organization.

Thus, the middle-level official is much more than a passive executor of orders. He or she is a leader in action, a strategist in disguise, and a teacher in practice. The effectiveness of any organization hinges significantly on the competence, character, and clarity of those who stand in this middle tier. By understanding the vision, breaking it into achievable tasks, communicating effectively, monitoring sincerely, solving problems, supporting people, maintaining order, building bridges, reporting honestly, and learning continually, a middle-level official becomes not just a manager but a maker of success.

❒

Chapter-26

Fostering Self-Development among Top-Level Executives

Leadership is not simply about authority; it is about direction, inspiration, and responsibility. In every organization—be it a government institution, corporate setup, educational environment, or non-profit—the success of a team depends less on the resources available and more on the quality of leadership guiding it. A leader shapes the journey, removes obstacles, and ensures that the energy of the team flows cohesively toward a common purpose. Good results do not occur by chance—they are created through deliberate vision, thoughtful execution, and consistent nurturing. This article explores ten vital and systematic steps a leader must follow to ensure good results through their team, blending strategic thinking with human insight.

The foundation of leadership begins with defining a clear vision and mission. A vision answers the essential question: why are we doing this? It provides purpose beyond routine work and inspires people to see themselves as part of something larger than their individual roles. A compelling vision turns daily tasks into steps toward a shared goal. Alongside this, the mission clarifies what exactly needs to be done. Without a clear mission, even a motivated team can wander aimlessly. It is the leader's role to articulate both elements clearly—vision for inspiration, mission for direction. When these are communicated well, every member of the team finds alignment and clarity, and their efforts naturally converge.

Having defined goals, the next crucial responsibility is to select the right team members and assign roles effectively. Leadership is not about doing everything yourself, but about knowing who can do what and enabling them to do it well. Each individual brings a unique set of strengths, experiences, and aspirations. The leader must understand these differences and use them strategically to create a balanced team. A team of only thinkers without doers, or only doers without planners, is likely to falter. Diversity in thinking, skill, temperament, and background adds resilience to the group. A wise leader observes people closely, gives them the right opportunities, and occasionally challenges them beyond their comfort zone to unlock hidden potential.

After assembling the team, the next step is to create a structured action plan that translates the goals into daily and weekly tasks. This roadmap should not just list what needs to be done but also define how and when it should be done, who is responsible, and how progress will be reviewed. A good plan includes milestones, deadlines, and check-ins. However, more importantly, the planning process must involve the team members. When people contribute to shaping the plan, they develop a sense of ownership. Ownership fosters responsibility. Responsibility leads to higher commitment. Planning should never be a top-down imposition; it should be a participative process.

For the action plan to function, communication must be strong, frequent, and transparent. Leadership communication is not just about giving orders. It is about sharing context, listening to concerns, resolving doubts, and creating a space for honest exchange. A good leader communicates expectations clearly, listens without judgment, and ensures that team members feel heard. Regular updates, feedback loops, and informal interactions are essential. Silence breeds confusion. In the absence of clarity, assumptions grow, which can derail progress. Communication also creates a climate of trust, which is the bedrock of effective collaboration. When people know what is going on, they work with greater confidence and less hesitation.

Even the most well-structured teams can falter if their spirits are low. That is why the emotional tone set by the leader is critical. Motivation and inspiration are not luxuries—they are necessities. People need to feel appreciated, encouraged, and supported. A good leader recognizes effort, no matter how small. They celebrate small wins, uplift those facing difficulty, and protect the team from negativity. Conflicts, burnout, or demoralization should be addressed early. A leader's enthusiasm, integrity, and resilience are contagious. When a leader believes in the team, the team begins to believe in itself. And belief can often do what strategies cannot.

Monitoring performance is essential to ensure that plans do not remain on paper. However, this must be done without micromanaging. Constant interference or excessive control breeds resentment and reduces creativity. A wise leader builds systems to monitor performance—such as review meetings, performance dashboards, or informal check-ins—but also creates space for autonomy. The goal is not to control every action but to guide outcomes. When people are trusted, they tend to rise to the occasion. When they feel doubted constantly, they shrink into mechanical behavior. Effective monitoring balances freedom with accountability.

Every team encounters uncertainty. Plans go wrong. Situations change. Unexpected challenges arise. In such moments, the ability of a leader to make timely decisions becomes the deciding factor. A leader must remain calm, gather facts, consult relevant team members, and act decisively. Indecision can be more harmful than a wrong decision. Of course, a leader must not act impulsively, but neither should they get paralyzed by fear of error. When the team sees the leader take charge during confusion, it strengthens their trust. Decision-making also involves prioritization—knowing which battles to fight, when to push forward, and when to pause and regroup.

Accountability is not something a leader demands—it is something a leader demonstrates. A good leader takes full ownership of the team's outcomes. If things go wrong, the leader does not pass blame to individuals but shields the team, accepts responsibility, and then works within to resolve the issues. This earns immense respect. It creates psychological safety for the team and motivates them to give their best without fear of punishment. At the same time, accountability means addressing internal weaknesses with honesty. Mistakes must be analyzed not to assign blame but to learn and prevent repetition. A leader is the guardian of both performance and morale.

The final, but never-ending responsibility of a leader is to create a culture of learning and innovation. No team can remain static and succeed in the long run. Change is constant. Markets evolve. Technologies shift. Expectations rise. To survive and thrive, the team must keep learning, experimenting, and adapting. A leader must encourage curiosity, reward creative thinking, and treat failures as learning opportunities. When people feel safe to try something new, they often discover better ways of doing things. Upskilling should be a regular process, not a reaction to crisis. A dynamic team, led by a learning-driven leader, stays competitive, relevant, and motivated.

To summarize, great leadership is not about command, charisma, or control—it is about clarity, consistency, courage, and care. A good leader defines a vision, sets smart goals, builds the right team, plans thoroughly, communicates openly, motivates deeply, monitors wisely, decides firmly, protects responsibly, and fosters learning continuously. These ten practices, when executed sincerely and systematically, lead to not only good results but also a culture of excellence. Leadership is not an event. It is a journey—a day-by-day commitment to bring out the best in others, and in doing so, to become the best version of oneself.

❐

Conclusion

Personality development is not a one-time task but a lifelong inner journey. It cannot be rushed, forced, or externally imposed. It grows in a rhythm—step by step, layer by layer, much like a tree rising from a seed. In Indian philosophical systems, particularly Advaita Vedanta, Sankhya, and Yoga, there exists a profound understanding of the human journey: one that begins with the desire to evolve and culminates in liberation (*moksha*), the eradication of ignorance. Between these two ends lie many subtle and powerful stages: discrimination, dispassion, right intention, selfless action, concentration, inner wealth, and ultimately, freedom from ignorance.

1. Willingness to Grow and Evolve: The First Awakening

The first spark of personality development is the desire to grow. Without this inner call, no real progress is possible. This willingness is not born from social pressure or comparison—it emerges from self-awareness. A student may feel compelled to overcome laziness. A young professional may sense the need for better emotional control. A seeker might realize the limitations of material success.

Willingness is the birth of the seeker within. It sets the soul on fire. Until this fire is lit, no amount of knowledge, advice, or books can transform anyone. It is the stirring of consciousness that declares—*"I want to become more than I am."*

2. Discrimination (Viveka): The Capacity to Discern

Once the will awakens, the next crucial step is discrimination—*Viveka*. This is the power to differentiate the essential from the non-essential, the eternal from the ephemeral, the important from the trivial.

Discrimination is the light of the intellect that helps one make wise choices. Should I react with anger or stay silent? Should I chase pleasure or invest in long-term joy? Should I flatter to gain favour or stand in truth even if alone?

A developed personality does not react impulsively. It responds with clarity, guided by this inner discrimination. Viveka is the compass that keeps us from being scattered by desires, distractions, and false goals.

3. Dispassion (Vairagya): Detachment from the Unimportant

Discrimination must give rise to dispassion, or vairagya. Once we know what is important, we must stop craving what is unimportant. Dispassion is not dullness. It is wisdom-powered freedom from clinging.

Many personalities get stunted because they are entangled—seeking validation, hoarding possessions, obsessed with others' opinions. Vairagya loosens these chains.

A person with dispassion does not waste energy in envy or regret. They become inwardly poised. Vairagya gives one the freedom to act without dependence on outcome. It makes the personality deep, calm, and inwardly strong.

4. Doing the Work (Karma): Commitment to Action

Discrimination and dispassion do not mean renunciation of action. True growth begins when we engage with life responsibly. Karma—meaning action—is the next essential step.

To evolve, one must work. There is no bypass. One must study, serve, train, speak, write, lead, create. Personality is shaped not in imagination but in the field of action.

But what kind of action?

5. Intention: Selfish or Selfless

The motive behind action matters more than the action itself. A gift given for fame is not a pure act. A harsh word spoken in love is not violence. It is intention that shapes karma's impact.

Selfish work, even if skillful, creates inner restlessness. It feeds the ego and ultimately makes the personality fragile—dependent on praise, fearful of criticism.

Selfless action, born out of service, purifies the mind. It expands the sense of identity—from "me" to "we." The best personalities are those who serve a cause greater than themselves. Their intentions are clean, their work is rooted in dharma, and their energy radiates authenticity.

6. Concentration (Ekagrata): Inner Focus

As work deepens, the need for concentration arises. A scattered mind weakens personality. A focused mind sharpens it.

Ekagrata, or one-pointed attention, is a muscle that must be trained. Whether in speech, study, or leadership, the ability to be fully present defines a refined personality.

This is not mere focus on tasks—it is the ability to stay with an idea, emotion, or problem without drifting. Concentration reveals hidden insights, aligns thoughts with goals, and enhances efficiency.

In Indian traditions, meditation is the supreme tool to develop concentration. But even outside formal meditation, every act done with full attention becomes a mirror of personality maturity.

7. Sad-Sampatti: The Six Inner Qualities

Now comes the deeper inner development—called Sad-Sampatti in Vedantic tradition. These are six jewels of mental discipline that polish the personality from within:

- **Shama**: Tranquility or mastery over the mind.
- **Dama**: Control of the senses and outward actions.
- **Uparati**: Withdrawal from meaningless indulgences.
- **Titiksha**: Endurance of pain and hardship with patience.
- **Shraddha**: Faith in truth, self, teacher, and path.
- **Samadhana**: Deep inner resolve and single-mindedness.

These six traits act like six pillars. Without them, personality becomes a weak structure—easily shaken. With them, one develops grace under pressure, depth in silence, and integrity in action.

8. Liberation (Moksha): The Flowering of Self

The final and ultimate stage is liberation—not necessarily from the world but from ignorance, ego, fear, and inner bondage. This is not an abstract spiritual goal. Moksha is the natural result of complete personality development.

When a person is no longer driven by craving, no longer trapped by ego, no longer shaken by success or failure—that is liberation.

Such a person is calm yet active, inwardly free yet outwardly responsible, simple yet profound. Their personality is like a fragrance—it spreads without effort, uplifts without preaching, leads without dominating.

Liberation is not the end of personality; it is its perfection. It is the blossoming of one's highest potential, where one lives as consciousness—not just as a body or a name.

The Sequential Flow: Why the Order Matters

These eight stages are not rigid compartments, but they do follow a natural progression.

- Without **willingness**, there is no conscious and sincere movement.
- Without **discrimination**, there is no clarity.
- Without **dispassion**, there is no freedom of action.
- Without **right action**, there is no discipline.
- Without **pure intention**, there is no inner cleansing.
- Without **concentration**, there is no depth.
- Without **sad-sampatti**, there is no inner infrastructure.
- Without **liberation**, there is no fulfillment.

Each stage builds upon the previous one. Skipping steps creates imbalance. Jumping into action without discrimination leads to burnout. Practicing meditation without sad-sampatti leads to spiritual confusion. Talking about liberation without inner purity leads to hypocrisy.

Therefore, true personality development is like a ladder—each rung has its place, and only by ascending step by step can one reach the summit.

From Becoming to Being

In essence, personality development is not about acquiring skills alone. It is the gradual refinement of the self, until all that remains is pure being—radiant, calm, compassionate, and wise. The journey from **willingness** to **liberation** is not just a philosophical idea—it is a practical roadmap. Every human being can walk this path. Every child, teacher, leader, or seeker can ascend these steps, steadily transforming the raw material of life into the gold of a liberated personality.

❑❑❑

Notes

Notes